A JOURNEY OF COMPASSION

Letters from a Street Minister

A JOURNEY OF COMPASSION
Letters From a Street Minister

by Bill Lane Doulos

WIPF & STOCK · Eugene, Oregon

Wipf and Stock Publishers
199 W 8th Ave, Suite 3
Eugene, OR 97401

A Journey of Compassion
Letters From a Street Minister
By Doulos, Bill Lane
Copyright© by Doulos, Bill Lane
ISBN 13: 978-1-60899-003-0
Publication date 4/11/2016
Previously published by Lizardi Communications

DEDICATION

This book is dedicated to the people of Union Station and The Depot, the poor whom I have been privileged to love and serve for 15 years.

* * * *

Contents

Acknowledgements	ix.
Introduction	xi.
Oh, What a Feeling!	1
Wrinkled Healing Fingers	5
Working in the Gray Areas	9
Little Joe Is Dead	11
Victims of Reality	15
Coping with a Reservoir of Guilt	17
The Institutional Shuffle	19
Fury Has Its Day	21
Twelve Pack Ideas	23
Reversing the Downward Spiral	25
Overwhelmed by Do-Gooders	27
One of Our People	31
Chutes and Ladders	35
Keeping a Foot in Both Worlds	39
Putting a Cap on Greed and Violence	41
Using the Next Five Minutes	45
Deflating Hatred	49
The Ritual of Resurrection	53
A Grand Opening for Hope	55
Forgetting Things That Are Orange	57
Ministry in the Living Rooms of America	61
The Goodness of Creating	65
Leveraging a Little Bit of Truth	69
The Dream of Simply Living	73

The Liveliness of Truth	77
A Life That Is Fragile	81
Addiction to Duty	85
Seeking Christ in Others	89
Charity Is Who You Are	93
The Sacred Chair	97
The Seductions of Sharing	101
The Miseries of Christmas Eve	105
The Mysteries of Christmas Day	109
The Poor and the Potential for Greatness	113
Finding the Shape of God	117
Our Silent Successes	121
The Aspirations of the Poor	125
A Journey to Skid Row	129

Acknowledgements

I wish to acknowledge several groups of people who have directly or indirectly inspired this book, because they have inspired me.

My colleagues on the staff of the Union Station Foundation are the most splendid group of social service providers. Their commitment to the poor is exemplary.

My colleagues on the staff of All Saints Church, where I currently serve as Associate for Urban Ministry, and the people of the wider All Saints Parish, have been a constant encouragement to me for 15 years. I am challenged by their example of discipleship, and by the prophetic vision of my Rector, George Regas.

The board members and volunteers who work weekly and monthly at Union Station and The Depot, our outreach to the hungry and the homeless, are the backbone of our ministry. Our volunteer staff has grown to 250 people, from many congregations and from the community at large. They prove that common folk engaging in obscure and routine acts of compassion can change lives.

Our Union Station donors, including over 2000 individuals and 40 congregations, have allowed our ministry to grow from a staff of one and a storefront that rented for $100 a month when we began in 1973, to a staff of 15 and a beautiful new facility. I am flattered by the thought that more social work and caring take place in one day through our current outreach than I was able to carry out in one month in our beginning years.

My new employer on Skid Row, the Church and Temple Housing Corporation, combines the talents and commitments of two remarkable congregations—All Saints Church and Leo Baeck Temple. I am grateful for the pioneer ministry they have invited me to lead.

Jim Baker, my business partner in Twelve Pack Enterprises, a for-profit venture in ministry that involves the private sector in social service investments, shares a vision with me of a world that is more just because of the potential response of capitalism to human need.

Finally, my mother and my daughter, with their wisdom and insights, are often in the background of these letters. The love of God is focused on me through them.

Introduction

When I began to work at Union Station in 1974, I had no idea of the journey I was undertaking. What began as a one-year commitment of modest dimension has become a consuming passion to be with and for the poor, and to engage the compassionate and resourceful people of faith in work with the poor.

I have personally experienced more of God's mercy than I thought existed in the universe. I did not know that I was capable of the dedication that I have displayed. I am grateful for the blessings of health and relative sanity, for family and nation, for the privilege of belief. These are "interim" blessings, to be enjoyed one day at a time, and not to be taken for granted. My work at Union Station and The Depot has given to me a mission which has carried me beyond the bounds that I originally set for myself.

Now when I look out onto the Skid Row streetcorner below my window I see people dying from abandonment and loneliness. A man urinating in public has just fallen over in the parking lot outside my door—just when I was gazing outward for a symbol of the urban crisis that confronts church and society. Now he makes his way unsteadily northward, and because my vision is framed by a window three feet across I cannot tell where he came from or where he is headed. The tragedy is not the misdemeanor of public drunkenness, but the felony of anonymity. In a world that was created by God as a showcase for community, this child is unknown to the caring community of faith.

The urban crisis that he represents is at heart a spiritual crisis.

And it is as much my spiritual crisis as his spiritual crisis.

And so this book of letters—capturing my thoughts as a participant in ministry to the poorest of society's poor, reflecting my journey to Skid Row where I presently live, embodying my hope that the ingenuity and faithfulness of God's people can transform my own life, and life as it passes by my window—this book of letters is offered to help you on your own faithful journey.

One of my great privileges in my work has been the privilege of keeping a foot in two worlds, the world of resources and the world of needs. There is no other way to do ministry. If you stay forever in the world of endless need, where is the solution? And if you escape forever to a world apart from the very real crises of our age, where is life's meaning? So the greatest revelation of my ministry has been this very simple and apparent truth, that the rich and the poor are both important to God's Kingdom. And parallel to this reality is the reality of a mutual ministry: The poor need the rich; and the rich need the poor. The Union Station and Church and Temple organizations that I serve are rooted in this conviction.

I am a broker between these two worlds. I love to be at home with the powerful people of our society, to enjoy their world and to count myself as a beneficiary of its goodness and beauty. Yet I also love to be among the poorest of the poor. My life is also immeasurably enriched by these children of God, hanging on to the bits and pieces of hopefulness and order that infiltrate their lives.

These letters, written over the past eight years, express

some of the thoughts about meaning and the quest for meaning, beauty and the longing for beauty, that have emerged from my work. I hope these thoughts are helpful to you as you find your own place of work and ministry. I pray that they will lead you to deeper and more hopeful involvement with both the rich and the poor of our society.

Our world is framed by the emerging crises of homelessness and hunger, addiction and disability, loneliness and mental illness, ignorance and unemployment. Our families are dissolving and our inability to articulate our human values is symptomatic of our lack of values. I have seen these enemies to God's created order; I live among them; I have not solved the crises.

Yet I am filled with hope and confidence. I have also seen the Spirit of God at work in our age. I have seen the people of God, as frail and nervous as I am at times, create oases of caring after the fashion of our creator God. It is not so much the impact of our efforts, although that can be substantial, as it is the link with the Spirit of God that gives me hope.

So as you engage the realities of despair that emerge from these stories, I hope you also sense the victory of God.

Bill Lane Doulos
June 20, 1989

Oh, What a Feeling!

Christmas, 1982

I have noted occasionally throughout my life the gratification that comes to people through working at Union Station. I know that many of you share in this experience through your own commitments and involvement.

Being involved with the poor on behalf of Christ and Christ's Church is a mysterious phenomenon. I know there have been times this past year, especially as the number of needy people in our community has risen and their situations have become more severe, when I have been drained and frustrated. Yet as the year reaches its climax, the sense of despair fades and the occasional joys become the overarching reality.

Despite the turmoil and disappointment and trials of discipleship, the author of James (1:2) encourages us to "count it all joy!" This is a fantastic admonition, but it is not fantasy. It is simply mystery.

You have probably had that puzzled feeling at the end of the month when, despite your budget and your careful accounting, you don't know what's happened to all the money you thought you had. There is mystery here. Sometimes I say this to myself daily: "I thought I had $20 in my pocket when I left home this morning, and I know that now I'm, unaccountably, broke. I can't remember spending all of that, I don't have anything to show for it, and I wasn't robbed." This muttering is usually followed by a deep sigh!

As I retrace my steps during the year, I realize I have been involved in many disappointments. Personal interaction with people at the Station does not always bring desired results. Situations have stubbornly persisted. Some people have come to see us and been substantially helped and gone on their way; more have come to us, been fed and befriended, but are still on our doorstep—hungry and lonely victims of self and society. I don't take their plight lightly. I think of Jesus and remember that he was born as an outcast and died as an outcast in his society.

Yet as I recount the gains and losses of this year, the abiding sense, amazingly, is all joy and privilege. I know I have given, but I am unaccountably rich. I have been a servant in small ways, but I think of myself as more of a king. I have experienced despair, but I am filled with hope. I have lost some of my life to frustration and ineffectiveness, but I feel downright victorious!

Shall I check myself in at the nearest mental health facility?

Or shall I go to church on Christmas Eve, kicking my heels high like that fellow in the Toyota commercial? "Oh, what a feeling!"

(Feelings are not bad, and they may persist throughout the year, and worshipping at Christmas is not bad, either, and may similarly become habitual.)

As you recount your own stewardship of your own life, may you experience this same mystery. The Christmas Eucharist, as we celebrate the brokenness of Christ, is as close as I can come to explaining it. For me, this is where the mystery focuses itself: the birth of the one who gave his life away... and found it.

Though it may not be appropriate behavior at the high altar rail, may you, in your own way, kick your heels high this Christmas. And may you keep on kicking throughout the year to come.

Wrinkled Healing Fingers

March 4, 1983

"I have all the comforts of home, except the home!"

This was the spontaneous statement of one of our Union Station patrons recently as he reflected on the fact that all of his considerable belongings were now in storage while he himself had no place to live.

Having no place to live is beyond imagination for most of us. For many of our brothers and sisters around the world it is reality. And for increasing numbers in Pasadena it is also reality.

We have always been aware of a handful of local homeless citizens, and in some cases throughout our Union Station history we have come to the rescue. There was the 70-year-old man living in a backyard shack who didn't know his age and poverty qualified him for Supplemental Security Income, a $450-$500 per month allowance. There was the 77-year-old woman suffering from senility who sat on the bench outside the YMCA at night with uncashed Social Security checks in her purse. There was the elderly gentleman who sold his home to a con artist for $1 and thus would have been homeless, except that Union Station and Police Detective Dennis Peterson intervened to undo the wrong.

And there have always been a handful of hard-core street people, whom we have been less able to help, who have preferred to bed down in the parks or bushes.

But we have a new phenomenon in Pasadena these days. Fourteen people live in an abandoned and condemned apartment building. Seven others live in a burned-out house. A couple from Texas have a hidden niche somewhere. Our recent survey revealed that 30% of about 150 regular patrons live out-of-doors or close to it. And most of these people are in their 20s.

I wish I could say that all these folks, and scores of other Pasadenans unknown to us, were simply victims of the economy. Then I could play upon your sympathies and blame some distant scapegoats—a cathartic exercise. And we could vote for different scapegoats next time around.

The problem is not so simple and the solution not so easy.

Some are naive enough to think you can have a war, then forge a peace and everything is back to normal. You can get away with cutting back on a child's nutrition for a while. You can have a recession, then an upswing in the economy undoes the damage. We talk about the scars that are left after these tragedies, when we should really be talking about the open wounds.

Union Station catches the fallout from wars, recessions, and a host of other individual and communal disasters. Our society is poisoned by that fallout for generations.

So when the politicians are all smiles with words about peace at hand and economy on the mend, Union Station volunteers are just beginning to work with the bitterness, the drug dependency, the alienation and apathy, the craziness and lostness, and the homelessness, that are spawned by everything from international insanity to family disjointedness.

I have been vaguely aware for a long time that my

work at Union Station, where I feel like I am picking up pieces of lives much of the time, makes me love my daughter more intelligently and intensely. It also makes me proud to be a faith partner with a young confirmand at All Saints Church.

Like E.T., we all can touch others with our little wrinkled healing fingers! And incredible joy and pride flow into our lives through these love relationships.

But, on the other hand, if we permit a child's educational opportunities to shrink and surround her with distrust, if we remove the symbols of hope from a young man's consciousness and let him have a nightmare of a world where the shape of a peace table is more critical than the lives that are lost while the discussion proceeds, if we build a bomb and close a library, then our children will grow up so spiritually and emotionally disfigured that we will live in fear of them.

There is no option but to continue to expand our involvement in work such as Union Station performs. What we accomplish in picking up pieces of individual patrons' lives is gratifying. But most of my gratification comes in a related way—because Union Station is a symbol of hope for our young people who wonder about our society's priorities. They wonder about the relevance of God. And they wonder about the role, if any, of the people of God, if any.

The fallout from war and recession is powerful. Almost as powerful as the hope that emerges from an act of love!

We underestimate the creative beauty and robust health that can grow out of a primitive work of caring such as Union Station represents.

Beauty and health are more alive among our patrons,

among our volunteers, and among those who from a distance simply know that models of justice and love still flourish. And our children, especially our children, will find inspiration and hope in what we do.

Our daughters and sons will do much better than we have done in caring for the dispossessed, but only because our work preserves a vision, floating in tattered but noble form over the otherwise ravaged landscape of our world.

Working in the Gray Areas

March 25, 1984

> "Some people hope for a miracle cure.
> Some people see the world as it is."
> —Billy Joel in "An Innocent Man"

And some people work in that gray area between these two extremes.

To simply hope for a miracle cure, or even to diligently pray for it, does not do justice to our faith traditions. People of God have always done more than hope for miracle cures for social problems. Poverty, war, homelessness, hunger, injustice, loneliness, discrimination, ignorance, disability—all of these interrelated dilemmas confront us today, and the "miracle cure" approach is tempting because it is so clean and comprehensive. And it puts the burden on God, the source of miracle.

There is too much escapism and "passing the buck" here.

Yet to "just see the world as it is" is an even more impossible approach. Many of us, I trust, cannot live with this status quo option.

My personal feeling is that when Jesus spoke of the "greater miracle" that would come to the world after his ascension, he was referring to the ongoing miracle of the church at work—individuals joining forces to address human need, occasionally at the cost of martyrdom, frequently at the level of personal sacrifice. While I do not view myself as one who has made any heroic sacrifice, I do believe I am part of this procession of humanity reaching out to the neediest of our brothers and sisters.

The real shortcoming of the overnight "miracle cure," as much as we at times yearn for it, even weep in its absence, is the fact that such a divine intervention would short-circuit our personal participation in the life of Christ. No matter how marginal that participation is, just to touch the hem of his garment breathes life into an otherwise mundane existence.

God has done God's work and calls us to ours. I am grateful to share in the work of Union Station. We don't see many miracle cures there, but we at least bear witness to that tradition of refusal to "just see the world as it is."

In whatever way you are involved with the healing of humanity, I hope you find some fulfillment as you work in the gray areas. The return we receive from the giving of self transcends our meager offering.

Little Joe Is Dead

May 1, 1984

> A 43-year-old man was fatally stabbed late Thursday night after an altercation with another man. According to Pasadena Agent Lee Baroni, William J. _____ was stabbed in the chest and neck with a steak knife during an altercation at 69 N. Catalina Ave. at 11:09 p.m. The victim left the building and ran a short distance before collapsing. Police patrolling the area arrested a 24-year-old man who was in the building where _____ was stabbed. _____ died later at Huntington Memorial Hospital.
>
> —Pasadena *Star News*

"Little Joe is dead."

These were the saddest words during a week of sadness.

We had known Billy for several years as "Billy"—loud, flamboyant, musically gifted, obnoxious, with an unrelenting propensity for self-victimization. He was a child of the streets. He had been in and out of scores of jails (mostly for shoplifting) and hospitals (for mental illness). He was one of the few people we ever had to ban from Union Station, because he left so much uproar and violence in his wake that we could not cope with him.

Yet he still called me several times a week, came in and out of my office at All Saints regularly. We still maintained a relationship with him, although his enormous emotional need was greater than we could meet. Our banning of him was not a judgment against his person, just a sober realization that we could not sabotage our entire ministry for the sake of one wayward child of God.

This is what his parents must have felt when they parted company with Billy. I have no doubt that they loved him, but the dull ache of separation from their only child was preferable to the daily destructive disruption that he visited upon them.

When I finally located Billy's family, thanks to an uncommon last name, some clues from a friend, and the help of some east coast telephone officials, I found myself speaking first with one of Billy's aunts. I made sure I had the right party, before I shared with her the news. Then she turned away from the phone and I could hear her say to her husband, "Little Joe is dead."

I had never thought of Billy's other life—his life as an infant, as a school child, as "Little Joe." When I spoke by phone with the man who was "Big Joe," Billy's now 70-year-old father, I was struck by how instantly he knew how long it had been since he had seen his son: when Billy was 26, 18 years ago, Mr. Joseph _____ had flown to New York to bail him out of jail. How much he and his wife now wanted to make things right. All their parental instincts thwarted and repressed for decades! How sad they were!

Oh the mountains of alienation that we live with, and that poison our world! At Union Station we try to chip away at the barriers that separate people from their families, from their peers, from God, from health and fulfillment, from the basic goodness and rightness of life as it can be, as some of us know it to be.

Works of mercy, such as Union Station, are based on the principle that there is enough food and shelter to go around. There is sufficient room on our planet, and plenty of pure water beneath its surface. Potentially there is enough skilled caring to cope with life's natural infirmities. The bread and the wine of the eucharist are never depleted. And surely there is enough pent-up love to bathe all of us continually in its elixir.

Would that we could release and distribute all that God has entrusted to us. We cannot afford to remain on the sidelines in this age-old effort to enfold all of God's children in God's goodness.

Billy's life and death were so costly to us. In his waywardness he drained millions of dollars from our society. I'm not sure what we or his family could have done differently. But I do know that we all would have been better off financially and emotionally, had we been able to reach him.

Union Station provides some peace and stability and security for those in need. Food and shelter and friendship tend to create an environment in which good things can happen.

We are relatively small and statistically insignificant, I suppose. But we maintain our outpost, for the sake of the few sons and daughters God has brought to us.

Victims of Reality

September 10, 1984

People who are governed by "appearances" are seldom the leaders or redeemers of society. They are too victimized by the dictates of "reality."

In this political season, I don't mean to add unduly to the confusion of ideas, so let me explain.

An anonymous commentator recently said about some of our Union Station patrons: "Why don't they get off their duffs and get a job?" This is sometimes an apt comment—we have said it ourselves to a few of our patrons, after we have come to know them. But the knee-jerk response to people and their plight is usually off-target.

People of faith and people who engage in works of mercy try to see beneath the surface and make their contribution on the basis of what might be rather than what is. We start with appearances but quickly go beyond them. We refuse to accept the "reality" of thousands of mentally disoriented people helplessly wandering our streets forever, of millions of our own citizens accepting the normalcy of hunger, of tension and terror as the status quo for our world.

Among our patrons, we might say that beneath the surface of Herbert's life there is sanity; within Alberta there is sobriety; deep down, Arnold is a motivated human being; Robert's gratitude is masked but not obliterated by his ingratitude. And beyond the cold war rhetoric there are two peoples yearning to tolerate and even embrace each other.

Our modest mercy is meant to draw out these more profound possibilities, without being naive about the barriers to their expression. The deepest reality is the Kingdom of God potential within each person's life. The Kingdom of God means health and wholeness, love and fulfillment. An application of mercy from without does wonders for the Kingdom of God within.

At The Depot overnight shelter and at the Union Station hospitality center we are in the business of unlocking buried treasure chests of goodness and humanity. The common bond between the oppressors and the oppressed, between the victims and the villains, between the rich and the poor, (and I personally find myself in all six of these categories!) is that all of us bear within ourselves these treasures of ideal human expression. We are all children of God.

Faith in the inner beauty and potential of ourselves and of everyone with whom we have contact is the stimulus that determines our response to the "real" world. We are motivated to lead that world, and to change it. May it always be so.

Coping with a Reservoir of Guilt

June 4, 1985

When you work with people like Ruth every day, as we do through our staff and volunteers, you can't afford the emotional expense of being horrified every time you hear about poor souls who sell blood for a living. Or about elderly women who have the RTD as a landlord. I would not last long in my job if I tried to save every "Ruth" who came to see me.

Yet I am not totally happy with myself, either. I keep a reservoir of guilt at arm's length, just far enough removed to permit me to function, to like myself, to be thrilled with the beauty of life and with the blessings of God, to make it to the next eucharist so I can confess my limitations.

And I also keep at arm's length a propensity for martyrdom—for that total devotion and sharing that would permit the challenges of life to overwhelm and consume me. I am no different than you: I have the capacity to give totally, without thought of preserving myself in the process. But for now I measure out my days and my scant devotion, content that at least the temptations of life have not yet overwhelmed and consumed me. I am happy that Ruth can still touch my heart.

I live in that gray area where almost all of us live—neither totally committed to others nor totally self-indulgent. At different times I am drawn to both extremes and play dangerously with both temptations. See how long you can hold your hand in the fire without getting burned; see how close you can come to the whirlwind without getting sucked in!

The art of being successful over the long haul in my career is to retain my health and humor and balance. During these critical times for Union Station, I feel I have to be successful. The day will come when my leadership will be expendable, and then I can live more dangerously.

Sometimes I am surprised (and happy) that people like Ruth don't ask me for more. She asked for $5. Doesn't she know the example of Jesus, the claims of God upon my life? Why didn't she ask that I treat her as I would my own mother?

I feel a great kinship with others of you, and I know there are many, who struggle with these questions and forego the easy answers. Your partnership with me in the journey of compassion is a great joy.

The Institutional Shuffle

August 19, 1985

As always, working with the poor is a mixture of hope and despair. Through these occasional letters I try to share with you some of the signs of each, knowing that it is a help to me to do this, whether it is beneficial to you or not!

Our friend Ralph Legg was murdered early one morning as he slept outdoors. It's hard to know which was more tragic—his life or his death. In the world of hunger and homelessness, often the poor prey upon the poor. We held a memorial service for him, attended by some of his relatives and Union Station friends.

Another patron made a serious attempt at suicide. Actually, he had only been a patron for about an hour, having been dropped off at our doorstep by another local agency. If it had not been for our staff member, Richard Carson, and the Pasadena Paramedics, he would have undoubtedly bled to death. He was homeless (except that we had just admitted him to the Depot for two weeks). He had no friends, no money, and was cut off from contact with his ex-wife and children. The day before he came to us he had passed out from not having eaten for three days. He had been unable to find a job. Within 24 hours after his suicide attempt, he had been transported to four different institutions—three hospitals and a residential care living center—what we call the institutional shuffle, one of the greatest causes of despair among the indigent.

We often wonder at Union Station where these people come from, what convoluted journeys bring them to us, what happens to them when they leave us and we lose touch, as we often do.

The signs of hope at Union Station are usually not as dramatic as the signs of despair, but that doesn't mean they are less powerful. One of our friends who is disabled and living in a board and care facility has been out of touch with his family for twelve years. But Les Bull of our staff was diligent enough to find a relative listed in a Colorado phone directory. A long-time patron whose public behavior was so bizarre that for years he was known by hundreds of Pasadenans who observed his benign craziness now has a full-time permanent job. With the help of some medication, he has held this job for about four months now. Everyone knew his craziness, but at Union Station we also knew his name, his history.

Calling someone by name—an approach that Jesus used so often—has a restorative and redemptive impact, especially among those who are accustomed to impersonal file numbers, cruel stereotypes and shunning. So we think we played some role in this man's "resurrection."

Signs of hope come from among the ranks of our volunteers, as well. I can think offhand of a couple retired individuals whose work behind the counter at the Station has brought them gratification. This is a kind of "resurrection" also—a bringing to life of instincts and capacities for caring that all of us have but that sometimes remain unexpressed.

Some of us have more compassion than we have opportunities to express it. And some, like myself, have more opportunities than we have compassion. Perhaps we should all get together!

Fury Has Its Day

September 16, 1985

There are few times in life when we can target injustice, can get it squarely and cleanly in our sights. When we do, we rise up and shout, "This is wrong!" The situation is no longer ambiguous for us. For clear-thinking and fair-minded individuals, these opportunities for pure righteous indignation are infrequent. Our world is too complicated. Most issues seem to be 51-49.

These close call issues add to our frustration. We know there is something wrong. We are true human beings for whom injustice is abhorrent. Like a hunter who hears a rustling in the trees, we yearn for a clear shot at our prey. One squeeze of the trigger relieves hours and days of waiting and stalking.

Some of us see injustice "clearly" too often. We shoot at the wind. We haven't learned to bide our time. At the other extreme are those who need to see a deer stop and pose before they can raise an emotion. Some are aggressive pursuers of injustice—constantly trying to focus in on evil; some wait for the deer to stop near the cabin.

Even Jesus, with his uncanny perceptions of human motivation, was infrequently the model of righteous indignation. But woe to the Pharisees and moneychangers who emerged from the shadows and ventured into his line of fire.

Human fury is awesome when it is unfettered by doubts.

The alleged "Night Stalker" has had a taste; the system of apartheid has perhaps received a fatal dose of fury. Thank God that fury still can have its day. Our humanity and our civilization are cleansed and preserved.

The yearning for civilization is one of the most abiding human instincts. Some day soon nuclear madness will be seen as a supreme threat to this instinct. Some day hunger and homelessness will be seen as a threat. Those who sight these evils before the masses do don't need to convince the rest of us so much as they need to bring things into focus.

Some day we will clearly see a child running in terror and we will say, "This is wrong!" Some day we will see a family picking through a garbage can and an uncommon resolve will take hold of our lives. Phenomena that have existed for ages suddenly are no longer 51-49. Ideological murkiness fades.

God's most fervent wish for God's people is not that they would become righteous. We would not be children of God if we were not already innately righteous. Blindness, which Jesus spent so much of his energy to cure, is the culprit more than malice is. Vision enables us to unleash the righteousness within.

At its highest level, my job with regard to hunger and homelessness is to show people that it exists—as vividly as possible—and then present a constructive alternative. Union Station and The Depot are not selfless endeavors. We are a band of people who see hunger and homelessness as wrong. We put aside political and ideological subtleties for the sake of engaging in a struggle that we know is just. There aren't many certain battlegrounds left to us, so we happily choose this one, striving to cleanse and preserve a civilization that has been good to us and to our children.

Twelve Pack Ideas

November 4, 1985

When you bury your head and your heart in your ministry, you face the great danger of working out of your past, never lifting your eyes to the horizons of new possibilities. Lethargy is a special threat when you work with more than your share of frustration and are occasionally jolted by disheartening news.

An antidote to such developments is to become more aggressive and expansive. How can we do our work of providing shelter and food better? What new ideas can we implement? This approach is the opposite of the "turtle" syndrome of defensive withdrawal. Human beings are not turtles, and I, for one, am most subject to discouragement when I am standing still.

I like to call new ideas "twelve-pack" ideas. There is a great comedy classic called *One, Two, Three*, starring Jimmy Cagney. He plays a Coca-Cola executive in West Berlin, and in one scene some crazy and innovative ideas are being suggested for breaking into new markets. A new convert to capitalism shouts, "We must go beyond the six-pack, to the twelve-pack!"

They may be a bit impractical, these "twelve-pack" ideas. But for centuries the church has been doing only passable work with the poor. Our great motto is, "The poor you will always have with you," and there's not much inspiration there. So perhaps it is time to entertain some new ideas.

What about a church where rich and poor worshipped and worked together? What about a city where the poor were not only tolerated, but where business and government took pride in serving the neediest citizens instead of wishing and developing them away? What about shepherding the poor in a careful way into our lives and homes, beyond what can be done at Union Station and The Depot, beyond the "six-pack"? We need some breakthroughs. We need to counter the dramatic downward spiral in the lives of so many of our brothers and sisters. We need to bridge the polarization prevalent in our world of the rich and the poor.

In addition to serving food and providing beds, we need to wonder. I have added a new line to my job description: "Dream!"

Reversing the Downward Spiral

January 10, 1986

> "I'm somethin', and I hope you think you're somethin' too!"
> —from "Celie's Song," from the movie *The Color Purple*

> "Put your arms around yourself."
> —George Regas, Christmas Eve Sermon

In the morning paper I read a report in which Emory University obstetrician Dr. Robert Hatcher says that lack of self-respect is hazardous to your health. I'm not surprised.

A common phenomenon among street people, in my 12 years of observation, is lack of self-respect. The "me first" generation, with all of its pluses and minuses, has largely passed by a segment of our population, where "me last" is a more common sentiment. Certainly there are those even among the poorest of the poor who are aggressive and self-assertive, and sometimes to an obnoxious degree. But discouragement and resignation are written on many faces at Union Station.

People don't believe they are somethin'. They don't embrace themselves with enthusiasm. This is the tragic shortcoming in many lives, producing more blight in the soul than is produced by lack of food or shelter. Feeding and housing people is easier than instilling the child-of-God dignity that ought to form our self-perception.

What we discover regularly at Union Station is that tending to the physical necessities indirectly tends to the soul as well. People feel warmer about themselves, are more secure about their place in the universe when they are literally warmer and more secure. Conversely, go hungry and homeless for even a few days, and watch the sense of dignity erode and the hope slip away. Then watch the patterns of behavior change unconsciously to reflect an anti-God, anti-social attitude. This scenario isn't guaranteed (there are heroes and heroines who overcome sustained deprivation), but the tendency is unmistakable.

Working against these downward-spiral realities are simple smiles and friendliness, using people's names, holding them accountable for their actions, maintaining discipline, providing food and shelter. Expensive commitments are involved here that lead to patient hard work. And patterns of thinking and acting and believing change.

If I did not believe this, I would not stay in my job one more day. (There are some days I don't believe it, so I usually make these career decisions monthly to allow for fluctuations!)

Overwhelmed by Do-Gooders

February 10, 1986

Union Station has always been rich in volunteers.

Today there are about 150 who are on our boards and committees, who work at our hospitality center three hours a week or at our shelter one overnight per month. I used to know all our volunteers; now I can't keep up with names and faces, churches and backgrounds, theologies and motivations. I'm just glad they all come to serve in the traditional Union Station ways.

If we paid them all $5 an hour to work for us, our annual operating budget would zoom from $180,000 to $300,000!

There is a newer breed of volunteers who also want to work for us, often in non-traditional ways. I have never before been contacted by so many people who want to devote their professional skills to help. They don't like the idea of people being homeless and hungry and despairing in a world so rich in resources and promise. They do like the idea that their community could become a place of human fulfillment for the downcast. They sense that God has given them gifts to use.

In recent weeks, for example, the following people came forward: an artist, two photographers, a jazz musician, a stock broker, a lawyer, an auctioneer, a health care administrator, a newspaper publisher, the head of a hospital emergency room, a cadre of poets, a judge, a bookkeeper, the director of a team of paramedics, a psychologist, a real estate agent, a nurse and a fundraiser.

Just think what our budget would be like if we had to pay these folks their usual fees!

I have had to become a broker, a middleman of sorts. My job is to take the compassion and skills these men and women offer and make them available to needy people and to sometimes desperate situations. Even though there is plenty of need to go around, it is not always easy to make a good match. You can't just link people up willy nilly. You have to make sure that both the provider and consumer of services have a satisfying experience. This is hard work.

These days when I get a visitor or a phone call, I find myself hoping that it's someone who wants to borrow some money, rather than someone who wants to take me out to lunch! I'm thinking of getting an unlisted phone number and only giving it out to poor people!

Some of you wonder why I don't get discouraged providing ministry to street people. How can I get discouraged when you all are sending me notes and money, showing up for your shifts at the Station and The Depot, and continually thinking of new ways to be helpful?

Give me a break.

Dealing with discouragement in the old days was a piece of cake compared to coping with this onslaught of goodness. The next time I send out a tear-off and a return envelope (at Easter) I'm tempted to include a box for you to check: "I have lots of time and skill and resources, but I don't want to share them this month!"

Except for one thing.

I was also visited this past week by another professional. He has a law degree and a journalism degree. He is a retired naval commander and a former board member (25 years ago) of a local charitable organization. Now 72 years old, he might have been another would-be do-gooder. But he didn't come to see me so that I could find a job for him to do. He came to see me because he is tired of sleeping in the laundry room of a nearby apartment building, tired of carrying an army blanket around all day, tired of not having a place to take a shower, tired of being wet and cold and hungry. I thank God he came to see me. The services you enable our staff to provide for him will give him a new chance to live the way he has almost always lived—with dignity and purpose.

So there is a job for all of us yet to do. And I guess we do need your services. I and my staff will just have to be equal to the growing task of helping find a niche for you. It's the opportunity I've always prayed for, the challenge I've continually presented to you. I just didn't anticipate that God and you would take me so seriously.

One of Our People

March 10, 1986

My 10-year-old daughter Melissa and I were driving down Colorado Boulevard recently when she spotted a person seated at a bus bench who was obviously homeless—"one of our people," as she calls them. This man had seemingly all of his earthly possessions in a few green plastic trash bags at his feet.

Actually, I didn't recognize the man as one of our Union Station patrons. There are a number of homeless in Pasadena who don't come to Union Station for food or shelter, prefering a more anonymous, independent existence. But I was happy to acknowledge that, yes, he was "one of ours." I was less happy about a block further on when Melissa suggested, "Let's go back and give him some money." I think she's going to be a politician when she grows up!

It isn't enough that unknown people come to me every day asking for my time or money. Now my daughter has me scouring the urban landscape for such folk!

Generally speaking, giving money directly to strangers in need is not good stewardship. But Melissa was insistent, and I had to balance normal operating procedure with the desire to promote her compassionate impulse. So I asked if she wanted to give him a dollar out of her allowance ("Yes.") and if she would also tell him about Union Station if he was interested ("Yes.").

I watched the animated transaction from the curbside, and the startled look on the man's face was worth the price of admission.

We are celebrating our Centennial this year in Pasadena. We have a great city—very diverse, very vigorous. Our new official slogan is "Where Happy New Years Begin." Yet this is also a city where poor people live out their lives 365 days a year. Poor people belong in Pasadena. I would not want them to have to go anywhere else. This is where we have the energy and the resources and the vision to work with our poor.

Our city and our people must make room for them. It will not happen automatically. In fact, the opposite will happen unless we hold central to our thought and work the needs of the poor. These needs include food and emergency shelter, jobs, low-cost housing, health care, education, friendship and spiritual expression. Are our institutions and people up to the task? If we are, then Pasadena will continue to be a great city.

Very few people who now live on the street were born into a "skid row" existence. The countryside and the suburbs as well as our cities have produced the people who now crowd into our urban areas. Hospitality centers and shelters don't create poverty, disjointed families, ignorance, ill health, drug abuse, mental disorientation, despair. We simply catch their victims as they drop out of the finer institutions of our land—victims of their own and society's shortcomings.

Often the people who flow into Union Station and The Depot, or who sit for aimless hours at our curbsides, have dropped out or been forced out of the same system that induces my pride and elicits my gratitude. I am well-educated, well-churched, well-governed, well-loved by my culture. Rather than curse this "system" that has served me so well, I prefer to broaden it to include the least of my brothers and sisters. I believe it can be done.

The creative ways must exist to enable the poor to live with dignity. Dignity is one of those intangibles that is enhanced the more it is shared. I live with greater dignity the more I enable the poor to do so. There's a lot in this for me.

Many of these enabling ways to promote dignity are undiscovered. At Union Station we are in the exploration business. We choose not to live with the skid row stereotypes and the track record of individual and social failure. Time and money and creativity must be appropriated, but we're going to make Pasadena famous! Some day people in far away places will say of our city, "That's where they care for their poor." "Yes, and don't they have a parade there, also?"

Where this journey of compassion will take us is unknown. But where it begins is clear. It begins with the question of a ten- year-old:

"Isn't that one of our people?"

Chutes and Ladders

April 14, 1986

    Chutes and Ladders is a rather straightforward board game. You roll the dice and advance the indicated number of spaces in an attempt to cross the finish line first. What makes the game interesting is its unpredictability. You may be far ahead, but if you land on a "chute," you can slide all the way back to "start." And you may be far behind, but if you land on a "ladder," you can quickly surpass your hapless opponent. You never know who's going to win or lose, despite the early trends, until you actually win or lose.
    If you play Monopoly, on the other hand, you can lock up the game early. Get all four railroads or Boardwalk and Park Place on your first several circuits of the board, and you can pretty much guarantee an eternal cash flow and the inevitable bankruptcy of the competition!
    Those of us who have established a positive early trend in our lives wish reality were more like Monopoly. Statistics tell me that I am a little over halfway through my earthly journey. And I have a few dollars in the bank, a good job, a lot of friends. People generally respect me. I still have my health and relative sanity and approximate faith. I have a couple of degrees, no criminal record, a decent credit rating.
    Not too shabby!
    But for all this positive momentum, there is no guarantee that I won't die penniless and friendless, in pain and dis-

honor. In fact, I may yet live most of my life this way.

There is a lot of darkness within and without that could defeat me. Other people or natural phenomena or world events could do me in, and if these external forces continue to bless me, there is always my own inherent potential to self-destruct. I am not morbid or fatalistic, but there are a lot of "chutes" lurking in my future.

Many of our volunteers and staff who work with the poor and the lonely know how fragile life is. Properly understood, the experience of life at Union Station will make you a grateful and generous person.

Why generous?

Because today a young mother in tears came to see me. I had never met her. But for a few moments I was her best friend. She is in danger of losing her three children to a foster home because she can't support them. Her husband has left her. I was able to give her some encouragement. She already knew intellectually what she could do, but life was nonetheless overwhelming. So I was generous with my time, because no matter how much life may rob me of my resources tomorrow, I know that today I seized the opportunity to share. For at least one day I was a successful human being. At least one person will remember me kindly.

What a privilege to play an important and constructive role in the lives of others! If you have that opportunity today, don't pass it up. You may not be able or inclined to be so generous tomorrow.

The greatest poverty that can afflict the human spirit is the loss of a generous heart. You will know that success has slipped away from you when your passion for helping others grows cold.

I hope you share with me the faith, rooted in your own religious tradition, that allows you to grasp your own life and the welfare of others in the same wide embrace. This is the philosophy that we put into practice at Union Station and The Depot. We bring together staff and volunteers who have grateful hearts and generous spirits with others who may be in desperate need. Transactions of caring take place every day and every night, and there is a mutual uplift.

In your own way most of you are part of this uplift. You contribute your volunteer time, your professional skills, your money, your food and clothing, your prayers and encouragement. At the end of each day, thanks to you, we just about break even—perhaps with a little encouragement left over to start us off tomorrow.

Keeping a Foot in Both Worlds

September 15, 1986

I was reading *The Wall Street Journal* (8/25/86) recently when I came across a front-page article about how federal funds for the poor had been diverted to a "redevelopment" project in Chicago that eliminated 210 units of substandard housing and built a total of 2,346 units of upper income housing. I fear this scandalous procedure might be followed in places a lot closer to us than Chicago, but the point of the *Journal* article is not the point of this newsletter.

The question I want to address, instead, is "Why does someone who works with the poor read *The Wall Street Journal*, anyway?"

Underlying this question is a basic misconception about the work of Union Station and The Depot. We have always had a unique goal among non-profit service agencies: We work with the rich and the poor, with the privileged and the underprivileged.

We have consciously chosen to bring these diverse groups together at our hospitality center and shelter for a couple of reasons:

1. These "diverse" groups really have a great deal in common. Everyone who is part of the human family has hopes and fears, opportunities and disappointments. We are all complex mixtures of good and evil, glory and

shame.

2. We need each other. The social problems that threaten to overwhelm our planet can only be solved if the rich and the poor can come together to lessen the fears and suspicions and strengthen the sense of worth and mutuality.

Both worlds are a bit scary and strange to me. Both groups are made up of fascinating and basically lovable people who, along with all of us, sometimes evidence unlovely outcroppings of self-defeating behavior.

So we keep a foot in both worlds. The work of Union Station and The Depot is to be present to both the rich and the poor (and to most of us who fall somewhere in between), to provide an opportunity to share and enrich each other's lives. We believe good things happen for both groups when people get to know each other without the pretense that tends to polarize.

Our interests are really mutual. Society can be just and life can be more rewarding for each of us if we work to make it better for all of us. And the alternative of polarization, if it goes unchecked, will surely destroy the abundant goodness of creation so that none of us survives to enjoy it.

Whatever the disparities of circumstance that separate us, we are convinced that there is at least enough food and basic shelter and potential friendship in our world so that everyone can enjoy the minimum daily requirement.

Putting a Cap on Greed and Violence

Christmas, 1986

At the conclusion of our October Enrichment series I asked the class to consider this question: "Do you think the day will ever come when homelessness and hunger will cease to be a problem in our American society?"

What is your answer to that question?

In other words, are we dealing through Union Station and The Depot with a social reality that will never change, or do we fully expect that permanent solutions can be found and implemented? If you ask me about less tangible problems, such as poverty and injustice, I tend to agree with Jesus that "the poor will always be with us," and to eradicate social injustice seems like an impossible dream. Not that we don't appreciate the value of the eternal struggle, and those who work in these arenas have my deepest admiration. But I personally like to get my hands on problems that have concrete potential solutions. The challenge is still huge, but it is not hopeless.

There is simply no compelling reason to tolerate homelessness and hunger.

Human nature, short of the final fulfillment of the Kingdom of God, has a dark side that will always find a way to express itself. Greed, envy, hatred, covetousness, self-pity and a host of other sinful tendencies strike at the heart of our ability to be fully human. But we don't have to implement our hatred, for example, with nuclear weapons. In primitive times people were content to express hostility through the use of clubs and stones. Is it too utopian to believe that someday soon we could be a bit wiser and more civilized in our sinfulness with regard to nuclear arms?

Similarly, we don't have to implement our greed by denying some of our brothers and sisters the right to food and shelter. The role of the enterprise we call civilization is to put a cap on some of the more grotesque expressions of human nature, and to unleash the creative beauty that marks us all as God's children. People of faith know that this wondrous beauty of all of God's creation will finally triumph, or else God is not God. We are also driven to express this beauty each day, or else we are not God's children. The ugliness of the nuclear threat and of homelessness and hunger fall outside the arena of reasonable sinfulness. They are intolerable.

In the past our society has dealt successfully with many great social problems: slavery has been eliminated, laboring men and women have a right to make a decent living, women have the right to vote. These traumatic changes to our culture were not easy to effect. The fact that we have succeeded in some well-defined ways does not make us a perfect nation. I simply believe that homelessness and hunger are two tangible challenges that can be met.

We will get to the mountaintop on these issues.

How much will it cost? That question has two answers:
1. A lot
2. A fraction of what it costs for us to maintain a society where families are homeless and children are hungry.

So I am not worried about the cost. The real question is whether we can capture the hearts and minds of the American people with the moral rightness of our cause. The "American people" is a non-threatening way of saying "YOU!"

Will you climb this mountain with us?

We don't want to order our society and we don't want to order our own lives in such a way that people in our neighborhoods are forced to say:

> "And homeless near a thousand homes I stood,
> And near a thousand tables pined and wanted food."

These words of William Wordsworth might have been appropriate to his generation. We do not wish them to characterize our own. The season of joy and giving is upon us, and God's challenge to us is fresh with each new Christmastide.

Using the Next Five Minutes

January 12, 1987

Often the work of Union Station and The Depot seems overwhelming. Two realities make it so.

First, the sheer number of people leads us to ask the question, "Where shall we begin?" The answer to this simple question has profound implications, because from experience we know that interest in and caring for the poor can often lead to dramatic results. Like a person surveying a desert wasteland, we know that wherever we choose to nurture and cultivate, the chances for the blossoming of human life increase. Sometimes our social workers tremble with the awareness that a poor person's fate lies so completely in our hands. We can't offer substantial help to everyone who comes to the door. Where there is so little hope and help, our assistance can make the difference between a person's continued downward plunge into the vortex of despair, or the same person's upward surge into renewed opportunity.

We use our good credit with God and with the volunteers we enlist to help us in our work to "master the possibilities." The fact that we have helped so many is a source of encouragement, but the fact that we have not even come to know so many others is humbling. We pray that these have been helped in silent ways beyond our knowing.

The second overwhelming reality is that so many of the lives we do touch are so complicated. We yearn for someone to come to our door with a simple need to which we can give a straightforward response.

I took my car into the garage last week with a simple need: a tune-up! But one thing led to another, and by the time the car was ready to be picked up I was surprised I recognized the beast. I asked, "What, you didn't paint it?"

Human souls and psyches are even more complicated than engines. People don't take care of themselves, sometimes for years. Life has taken some irreversible wrong turns. Union Station becomes the last stop before the salvage yard. And if human beings were not sparked by a divine energy, we would certainly consign them there.

What can we do in the face of these overwhelming realities?

I have been helped recently by a George MacDonald novel entitled *The Musician's Quest*. One of the social work heroines of the book is characterized this way: "As often as she gets hold of a poor, hopeless woman, she gives her a motherless child. It is wonderful what the childless woman and the motherless child do for each other."

All of us at Union Station and The Depot—staff, volunteers and patrons—are needy, and principally we need each other to fulfill our mutual potential. So in the midst of the complex needs of so many lives we remind ourselves that if those needs didn't exist we would have to create them in order to complement the configuration of needs that other lives present to us. The quiet quest for meaning happily greets the desperate plea for help, and lives are made whole on both sides of the counter at Union Station.

This is a crazy wisdom of God, but when you participate in it you begin to appreciate it. So as often as I go home from work and ask "Who needs this?" I hope to see my way through the overwhelming frustration to say, "I do!"

The hero of George MacDonald's book, Robert Falconer, must have dealt with the same question of where to begin a century ago:

> What I want is simply to be a friend of the poor. I bide my time...I go where I am led...In my labor I am content to do the thing that lies next to me. I await events. In all of life, there is nothing so significant as the next five minutes and whether we use it to do what God lays before us.

Deflating Hatred

February 9, 1987

> Lost in a haunted wood,
> Children afraid of the night...

That's how W.H. Auden described his society on the eve of World War II as he wrote the poem entitled "1st September 1939." Sometimes these words describe our culture today.

Last summer a poll of 1,254 adults in the United States found that only 36% believe that our children live in safe neighborhoods. And how many of us believe that we live in a secure world?

From my years of experience with people who are poor, hungry and homeless, I would use two words to characterize their prevailing state of mind: loneliness and fear. Sometimes those of us who are better off also struggle with the same realities, and much of life is spent trying to overcome the dual curse of isolation and insecurity.

When you are poor and on the street, the struggle becomes almost unmanageable. Usually these are people who have already experienced tremendous rejection. You can't lose employment, housing, family, friends or health without a chill permeating your body and your psyche. The poor person who is aggressive and violent is the exception rather than the rule. Most are docile and passive, and, as one rejection leads to another, the withdrawal becomes almost visible. Inwardness and alienation increase. Hostility supplants the normal inclination toward fellowship and sharing. And the people in our society who need the most help often create incredible barriers to separate themselves from readily available resources.

Much of our time at Union Station and The Depot is given over to penetrating barriers and reversing this aura of estrangement.

Sometimes on bad days I even feel alienated, surrounded though I am by friends and colleagues. When the light changes to "Don't Walk" just as I step off the curb I sense a personal rejection. How well would I cope if I missed a meal or spent the night outdoors? How long would it take for my facade of civility to dissipate into bitterness?

The "catch-22" of this scenario is that once civility is lost, then the people who associate with you really do begin to dislike you, and your imagined alienation becomes real. Some poor people I know go out of their way to give me reasons to dislike them and to separate myself from them. And I have managed over the years to cultivate a healthy dislike for a few. But more frequently I disarm their attempts at animosity with a persistent tolerance.

One of my patrons recently found reason to let the air out of all four of my tires. I instinctively knew who the perpetrator was, and I skirmished with my own bitterness, and I parked my car out of sight for a few days. But a week later I went up to him and thanked him (!) for not letting the air out of my tires *recently*. I robbed him of the one thing he was looking forward to most: the chance to protest his innocence. And I absolutely prevented him from ever contemplating such sabotage again. There is no thrill so great as the thrill of thwarting evil. Hatred is easy to come by, given all the reasons that we have for not getting along with people. But love is not frequently a knee-jerk, first-sight reaction. With love you have to be more cunning and creative. The people who defeat me are not the ones who do me wrong, but the ones for whom I cannot find a way to care. You are a fortunate person if love for others takes root and persists and abides, no matter what the provocation, and if hatred evaporates as the morning dew, when the slightest challenge is raised to its existence.

So Auden, understanding this inevitable triumph of love, was correct to climax his despairing poem with a stanza of hope:

> Defenceless under the night
> Our world in stupor lies;
> Yet, dotted everywhere,
> Ironic points of light
> Flash out wherever the Just
> Exchange their messages:
> May I, composed like them
> Of Eros and of dust,
> Beleaguered by the same
> Negation and despair,
> Show an affirming flame.

I like to think of Union Station and The Depot as places where mystical transactions take place—where the loneliness and bitterness of life are checked—where "the Just exchange their messages."

The Ritual of Resurrection

April 6, 1987

Resurrection is one of the great themes of religion and of life. It is a profound spiritual reality that finds confirmation in the routines of the physical world as well.

The coming of spring is a resurrection rite. It is not quite as dramatic here in Southern California, but in the blustery northeast where my home is one can almost feel the renewal of life as flowers bloom again and natural warmth returns to the land. That which was buried and forgotten reasserts itself.

The faithfulness of God is mirrored in God's created order. Belief in God is not a lonely spiritual journey into isolated fantasies about the way we wish things might be. The whole universe—where night turns into day so often and so naturally that we miss the obvious messages God sends to us—this whole universe participates with us as we celebrate the rebirth of hope and the resurgence of vigor.

God must have known what some of us could make out of our lives. The deadening routines. The numbing conformity. Some of us who hoped for fame settle for anonymity. Some who wanted to change the world struggle to gain control of their own circumstances. Some who were borne along by bright dreams in their youth now yearn for some slight sense of adventure.

The poor also find themselves at odds with the way life was meant to be. The dawn which was meant to signal another round of creative opportunity for work and relationship instead brings with it the awareness that nothing has changed overnight. "Where can I eat today? What is there for me to do? Where may I sleep tonight? Does anyone know me here?"

But resurrection is a theme among the poor also. The elderly woman (she would say middle-aged) who used to sleep in a movie theatre in downtown Los Angeles, whose feet became infected from neglect: she now sleeps in her own bed and sees our Union Station/Depot doctor every week. The young man who wandered the streets of Pasadena crazed and spinning and as if he had just emerged from the wilderness: he is now working and productive and restored. And others who are still victimized by disability and abuse can at least be in a place of friendship and nourishment. This too is a resurrection victory—when victims who may be their own worst enemies or who may be completely estranged from the world we know can at least find some warmth and acceptance.

The resurrection theme is never irrelevant. No matter how despairing the situations we encounter at our hospitality center and shelter, there is no life outside the reach of resurrection. We have learned the hard way not to give up on people. Some "hopeless" situations have been changed after we had given up, and they represent God's friendly reminder to us about our lack of trust in the ritual of resurrection. Springtime comes eventually to every seed we plant.

No matter what your circumstance is today—rich or poor, elated or anesthetized, in love with life or alienated by it—this is the appropriate season for rebirth. So trust this day and give yourself to its possibilities for growth and sharing.

A Grand Opening for Hope

May 6, 1987

At Union Station and The Depot we discover each day a new frustration—a new barrier that keeps us from easily achieving the goals we set for our work with our patrons.

Our organization is small and personal enough that we can actually set individual goals: Let's find a room off the street for Mary. Let's help John with his drinking problem. Let's find a job for George. Let's get Susan to take a shower.

Sometimes the goals are small, sometimes large. Sometimes we set them with our patrons, sometimes without their participation. On our intake form for our Depot overnight shelter we ask our guests to tell us what their goals are during their two-week stay with us. But for those who are mentally ill, anti-social, or users of alcohol or drugs, often the initial goal is to achieve their cooperation in some modest first step toward renewal. Few of our patrons are with us for very long without our staff trying to focus on a circumstance, a pattern of behavior that might be subject to change.

In a symbolic and intangible way, we hang a sign around each patron's neck that reads: "Reconstruction work in progress. Please excuse the inconvenience!" Or for some of you it might read: "Your Union Station/Depot dollars at work. Watch for our grand opening soon."

Of course, this approach to life ought to be true for all of us. We are all "in progress," and the great temptation for rich and poor alike is to become self-content and stagnant. Growth and change and maturation—physically, emotionally, mentally, spiritually, economically, socially—all of this process is so human that to forego it we have to forsake our birthright as children of God.

The poor are often so beaten down and overwhelmed by life that they are more likely to abandon the aggressive pursuit of change, even though they are the victims and losers within the status quo. But there is always an opening, however small, in the armor of apathy that deadens our senses. And our staff is vigilant. We are trained—more by God than by any book or teacher—to search out that glimmer of yearning.

The bad news is that frustration hems in the life of the poor 99% around. The good news is that with a 1% allowance for hope we can recreate the universe.

Wouldn't it be great if we had a little "grand opening" celebration whenever our patrons achieved some milestone of change? Joel found a room and is planting a garden in the backyard, and he's not interested in drinking anymore. Let's blow up a balloon! Jerry got some medicine for his infected foot. Have some punch! Carol is constructively participating in a class at church. Cut the ribbon!

Of course, we'd be celebrating all the time at Union Station and The Depot if we took notice of every slightest positive movement in people's attitudes and circumstances. Sometimes these "milestones" of change are more like "inch-pebbles"! Still, progress is progress, and every small opening that we find into people's lives is potentially a "grand" opening. So let's hang a banner: "Life is open again. Hope is back in business."

Forgetting Things That Are Orange

June 8, 1987

I was sitting next to my daughter, Melissa, in church last week. She had deposited her bright orange church school collection box in the pew rack directly in front of her, and it already had a few quarters in it. When I got up to leave, I whispered to her, "Don't forget your collection box," and she responded: "Oh, Dad, how can I forget it? It's orange!"

Where have I gone wrong as a father? How can my daughter, now just two years away from being a teenager, still think that human behavior manifests itself in such orderly patterns?

I wanted to stop and give her a brief sermon. I wanted to tell her about the basketball I had left at the playground once and about the time I came home from the market without the fruit that was at the top of my shopping list. I could fill a room with the orange things I have forgotten over the past 43 years.

There is a subtle philosophy afoot that claims that people naturally act in their best interests. We respond to all the compelling stimuli. We take advantage of all the readily apparent opportunities and pass by easily the doors that are marked "Do Not Enter." There are some gray areas, of course, where our human fallibility asserts itself, but for the most part we innocently follow a well-marked path, doing the things that naturally lead to goodness and prosperity and avoiding the obvious pitfalls. I envy you if you are able to govern your life by these simple equations.

But I want to tell you that kingdoms have been lost because people have forgotten things that were orange. Intricate and sophisticated plans have been produced by the finest human intelligence, only to lead civilization into the abyss because of some cataclysmic oversight.

If only someone in authority could ask, at the appropriate time: "Balancing the budget is fine, but should we really be cutting back on our children's opportunities for education?" "Self-defense is a noble goal, but do we want to produce weapons that can destroy the planet?" "Self-reliance is a wonderful concept, but can't we at least make sure that everyone has food and shelter?" "'Just Say No' is an effective slogan for an anti-drug campaign, but can we also provide bed space and counseling for those who want to escape addiction?"

These are complex questions for those who have been seduced by the pseudo-wisdom of some dizzying socio-economic theory. They have distant answers, usually coming at the end of labyrinthine arguments, for those who adopt some convoluted political analysis.

Too often in our society "professionals" answer these questions and leave us amateurs to live with the consequences. We should let the amateurs answer the questions and assign to the professionals the task of implementing the obvious, "bright orange" best interests of the people. Let the children among us answer the supreme questions .

What is true of civilization is also true of personal life. Think of the places in your life where you have failed. Were you done in narrowly by some slight mistake? Or did you "blow it" by a wide margin because basic and simple "bright orange" responsibilities were forgotten?

And think of what an extraordinary person you would be if you just carried out the ordinary duties of life with diligence: Honor your parents. Respect the dignity of others. Keep your commitments. Cherish your relationships. Care for the less fortunate.

These "bright orange" instincts are so much a part of human nature, though they may be buried beneath the weight of lesser inclinations. If we consistently obey our deeper instincts, we create a momentum for justice and morality that carries us toward a kind future.

And so I hope my daughter's generation can restore this momentum by remembering all the orange things I have been forgetting. I fear that she is too innocently trusting of her own instincts. But innocence can also be a virtue— perhaps the very one that is so necessary when men and women chart the course of civilization and determine their own personal agendas.

I do worry, though, about the people who assume that because we are an intelligent and progressive society we will automatically take care of all the "bright orange" basics. We will not, for example, let the gap between the rich and the poor widen to the point of global violence. We will never commit corporate nuclear suicide.

These dark possibilities—violence and suicide—are more real than we acknowledge them to be. And even as I yearn with my own life to enhance the opportunities for peace and justice in my world, I sense that I am stumbling. The basics have slipped from my grasp so often. Sometimes the orange things get lost in a blur of compromise and equivocation.

While I have quite a contribution yet to make, and I am young and strong and optimistic for a few more years, I am nonetheless eager to pass the baton to my daughter. While the orange still catches her eye.

In the meantime, I am able with others to create a good society. I will be more attentive to the simple requirements of life. In my work at Union Station and The Depot the mandate is very plain: Feed the hungry. Shelter the homeless. Encourage the disheartened. These have always been attractive and even compelling options for me. And I can never remember a time when the exercise of these options did not produce in my own life vigor and excitement, beauty and goodness, a sense of the eternal.

We would do well to pause and permit the bright orange compelling truths to present themselves again. It is strange how the opportunities for kindness and decency that place themselves squarely in front of us often lead to fulfillment, while we maneuver around them in search of some happiness that we think must be more elusive.

Ministry in the Living Rooms of America

August 10, 1987

Those of us who work at Union Station and The Depot have a philosophy of outreach to both the rich and the poor.

In attempting to have an impact on the problems we confront, we know we have to deal with whole people—people who have social, physical, spiritual and psychological needs. Our staff and volunteers can't simply deal with one narrow slice of people's lives. Every element of need and every possibility for growth are interrelated.

The fact that Mary doesn't have a place to live is related to her emotional health. The fact that John is hungry greatly impacts his spiritual well being.

Similarly, the destinies of all of us on this planet are intertwined. I cannot flourish as a human being until all of my brothers and sisters are fed and clothed. I cannot be a whole person until others are housed and educated. Perhaps this truth is not so self-evident to you. I would be hard-pressed to prove it. There is an element of mystery and faith here. We all have different gifts and varied potential for fulfillment. There will always be winners and losers in life, those who conquer the world and those who struggle just to survive. Yet my success is inexplicably diminished by another's failure. And my failure is ennobled by the achievements of my sisters and brothers.

Consider whether there is not great power in the notion that the obvious individualistic face of humanity is complemented by the more subtle expression of our commonality. Without denying the truth of my social and financial middle class status, I nevertheless sleep on the streets of Pasadena at night. I base my ministry upon this truth that I am united in suffering with the world's poor.

I don't know how to convince you of this reality. But I can point to the problems we have in society because we fail to appreciate the linkages that unite the greatest and the least among us. Our abilities to conduct war, to treat people as aliens, to segregate, to oppress, to discriminate, to enslave, to commit crime—all are predicated upon a lack of appreciation of our commonality. The great crime is the crime of condescension. We "descend" upon others because we fail to appreciate that they are our peers, our colleagues, our brothers and sisters.

So we must reach out to both the rich and the poor, and we must find better ways at Union Station and The Depot to sustain this outreach. I don't know if many other "soup kitchens" have this vision. Maybe we should just "stick to our knitting" and make sandwiches. But the religious community in America has been making sandwiches for over one hundred years now, since the early days of the industrial revolution when the urban poor became a social class. And despite massive efforts one could argue that today is the heyday of homelessness and hunger.

So we are trying something new. We are pioneers, pushing our way forward without too many answers. How do we express this commonality? How do we implement this vision? These are our challenges. This is the wilderness that we explore from our bold outpost at 202 N. Euclid.

This vision of universal well being must take us not only to ministry on the streets, but to ministry in the living rooms and schools and corporate offices and work places of America. Those who (write and) read this letter are just as much the mission field of Union Station/The Depot as are the hungry and homeless.

The Goodness of Creating

September 14, 1987

The sermon title of my priest, Denis O'Pray, was "Which Is Stronger: Evil or Good?" He raises one of the epic questions of the ages. The evidence of history does not point to an obvious answer.

So one is left with a choice dictated more by faith and function.

My faith says: "Good." I can support this choice by history as well as by daily experience, but I acknowledge that others can support the opposite choice in the same way. Faith, by definition, goes beyond the pros and cons of debate, and it goes beyond the whimsical nature of popular decision-making. For me faith is a solid, deliberative process of eliciting the answer to the question from within. When I say that "Good" is stronger than "Evil," I am saying more about the inner self than about the external evidence. I have consciously chosen to perceive humanity and the universe in a certain way.

Function also renders the verdict: "Good!" In other words, in order for me to function (and in order for civilization to function), I must believe that "Good" is stronger than "Evil." So the philosophical debate is over, although it is still enjoyable and stimulating. The point is, I must live my life as if "Good" were stronger in order for life to have meaning. "Good" is my home, my parent and my child. I must see my life as the offspring of goodness and the procreator of goodness.

Otherwise life deteriorates for me.

Part of being a child of God is being a "creator." When God looked at the results of creation—the stars, the earth, plants and animals, man and woman—God saw that "it" was good. The "it" here is not just the result of creation, but the process of creation. No wonder I feel "good" and "right" when I create something!

The process of creation is entirely dependent upon the goodness of life. So whether you're creating a work of art or a child or an evening meal, you're entering into the positive and good momentum of the universe. Evil is the process of destruction and good is the process of creation. Passivity is nothing more than evil in low gear; it is silent and subtle deterioration that in the end amounts to destruction.

To create and to heal and to preserve are basic instincts that contribute meaning and beauty to our existence. They are the antidote to much of the ugliness and boredom of our age.

As I left Union Station the other day, I ran into one of the most hard core street alcoholics who has ever come our way. He was in the patio sipping a cup of coffee, looking more alert and vibrant than I had seen him in a decade or so. Our art teacher, Lee Hill, had surprised me with a couple of his paintings just a few days before, so I took the opportunity to tell him how much I enjoyed his art.

"You didn't know I was a painter, did you, Mr. Doulos?" he asked with a twinkle in his eye.

Not exactly. But I knew, by faith, that you were a creator. I do know that you are a good person.

I didn't have the presence of mind to be so profound at the time, of course. I manage to save all my profundity for these letters without wasting any on my daily interactions with people!

But don't you feel "good" when you create something? Don't you feel "right" and "satisfied"? This feeling is not incidental or superficial; it is the daily expression of an eternal truth. It may not be a perfect painting or a perfect child or a perfect soufflé, but the mere act of creation places you peacefully in the midst of the universal flow of goodness.

The flow begins and ends with God, according to my theology. But whether you share that theology or not, I hope that you see your days and your relationships as creative opportunities. If you do, then you surely are among that army of people who believe that "Good" is stronger than "Evil."

Leveraging a Little Bit of Truth

October 12, 1987

Remember your high school algebra class when Mr. Fraley would tell you that it wasn't sufficient to know the right answer, you had to "show your work." You had to work through an equation that would produce the desired results. You could not intuit your way to an "A" in Mr. Fraley's class. In fact, he said it was better to come up with the wrong answer if you could only get the format of the equation right, than to record the right answer without the benefit of due process.

(I believe this was about the time when life began to be confusing for me!)

If we could just corporately close our eyes and picture a world in which everyone's basic needs are met and where people are living without fear—what a world this would be! We know this is the right answer, but how do we arrive at it?

In Mr. Fraley's class the easy part for me was knowing the right answer. I sometimes filled in the bottom line first. Then I would work backward and try to at least get close to the answer. If the answer was "7" and I could come up with an equation that gave me an "8," I would rejoice and arbitrarily insert a "-1" somewhere in the long line of numbers. Mr. Fraley is probably turning over in his grave right now, but he really did teach me a lot about life. I still use this "Doulos" method to balance my checkbook.

A long time ago I closed my eyes and imagined a City of Pasadena in which business, civic and religious leaders were joining with hundreds of grassroots citizens to provide for the needs of the poor. In the intervening years I have tried to figure out how to get there from here, and this has been the more arduous task. At times, in fact, when some business leaders vigorously opposed the relocation of Union Station to 412 S. Raymond, we were actually moving further away from the answer. But this ebb and flow is to be expected. Even when I balance my checkbook I frequently increase the margin of error before I sneak up on the truth.

Now things are more closely falling into place. Last year the Tournament of Roses Association asked us to sell their parade programs to raise money for the poor. All of a sudden there was a slight tie-in between people in immaculate white suits and others who wore rags. Not the Kingdom of God, mind you, but enough to insert in the equation which issues in the Kingdom of God.

Now the leadership of Old Town wants Union Station and The Depot to benefit from their "Old Pasadena Celebrates" festival on Thanksgiving weekend. A couple years ago when I talked with John Wilson he was asking me not to put our new facility within a mile of his Marketplace development. But a couple weeks ago he asked me, as a neighbor, to participate in a project of mutual support. This is called an "algebraic breakthrough" and if you get enough of these adjustments and can strategically place them in your equation so that you can leverage their impact... Well, the Kingdom of God is not far off!

You may think that I make too much of little things. After all, you protest, the general public still thinks of poor people as a bunch of bums. Government leaders still legislate against the interests of the weak. Business people still would like to ignore the plight of the homeless. And the religious hierarchy are often condescending and passive.

There are two reasons why I don't fully subscribe to the above statements. First of all, their judgments are too harsh. Secondly, they don't fit into my equation.

In my hometown of Pittsburgh the city planners once built what the media later dubbed the "Bridge to Nowhere." There are many bridges in Pittsburgh, and one evidence of literal shortsightedness is perhaps to be overlooked. It was a magnificent structure and served for years to instill a bit of humility and humor, both of which were needed at the time in local governmental affairs. The problem was, when you came to the end of the bridge you dropped into the Monongahela River.

There is enough data, I will grant you, to make a case for the indifference and hostility of people toward the poor. In a debate as to whether the world is good or evil, if you take the side of evil you can muster a lot of evidence, and I can muster perhaps only a little. But why do you want to win that debate? Wouldn't you rather leverage the little bit of truth in the notion that people are enlightened, kind and noble? Your "truth" doesn't fit into my equation. And when you come to the end of your concrete evidence, you drop into the abyss.

If you just deal with the raw data of life, without a vision, you will only be able to build a "bridge to nowhere." But if you have a bottom-line vision of a good society, you can make things fall into their purposeful place. You may have to massage and finesse and leverage, multiply and divide where appropriate.

I would rather begin with a good intuition than with a mountain of evidence. Then take a little bit of truth, carefully selected, and raise it to the "nth" power.

The poor are fed and housed, our citizens find encouragement and hope, and the City of Pasadena is a better place when we make the most out of a slight consideration. The ministry of Union Station and The Depot today is nothing more than a creative mixing together of 14 years' worth of individual acts of kindness. Think about that. Think about the role that you have played. Your own kindness has brought us close to our goal and sustained the vision. Thank you.

The Dream of Simply Living

January 20, 1988

Over the holidays I treated myself once again to the movie *Dr. Zhivago*. So much of the theme of this epic can be summed up in the yearning of Yuri Zhivago: "I simply want to live."

Whether under the Tsar or under Lenin, in Yuriatin or in Moscow, as a doctor or as a gardener—these "details" were relatively unimportant. One might persevere within any of these realities and create a place for "living." In the cottage outside Yuriatin, with ice and snow invading this unlikely home, Yuri Zhivago created such a place. Even the arch disciple of pure Bolshevik ideology, Strelnikov, tried to return in the end to satisfying the more basic dream of simply living.

What is this dream? To have a place. To be part of a family. To work and create. To know that one belongs to God. There is not much more to life.

We mistakenly think that such a scenario is too self-indulgent. We want to give ourselves to some great political or religious cause that takes us beyond ourselves. Causes have their place. But to be part of a family is to give to others. To work and create is to share oneself. To belong to God is above all else to be gentle, to open oneself to the world and to respond to its cry for help. All pure causes are rooted in these "self-indulgences."

As a doctor in war-torn Russia, Yuri Zhivago did not see

himself as a self-sacrificing hero. He did not work endlessly and without thanks out of some great political zeal or religious devotion. He was simply living.

Sometimes we make too much of politics and of religion. These constructs are meant to order our lives so that we can arrive at "a place" and enjoy "family" and "work. " As Strelnikov discovered, the transcendent causes and crusades are in the end unsatisfying. The quest for orthodoxy (political or, I might add, religious) is in the end defeating. The arrogance of the presumed rightness of belief quickly transforms ideology into a constraint rather than a construct, our master rather than our servant. Religion can get in the way of God's purposes for us almost as easily as it can help us to fulfill our human destiny.

There is something obscene about a society which does not allow its people to fulfill their basic dream. When we can say, in effect, to one of our sisters or brothers, "You don't have a place; no community of love exists for you; there is no work for you to do, " then we are also saying, "There is no God for you. " It is hard for us to know God in a vacuum, apart from God's tangible caring for us.

Atheism does not emerge from religious ignorance, it emerges from a disjointed society. Atheism means that God is not honored. God is not honored when people are homeless, unloved and idle.

Some well-meaning friends wish that I were more evangelistic. "Why not bring these poor, hungry, homeless souls to salvation?" they ask. Isn't it enough that I might bring one such soul to a place in life where God conceivably might be honored? There are 150 congregations in my community that can assist people to relate to God and to articulate their faith.

If it were not for these congregations, the ministry at Union Station and The Depot would not exist. This is a plain economic fact. Yet if it were not for Union Station and The Depot, the possibility for religious expression would be diminished in my community.

The Israelites asked a profound question out of the depth of their Babylonian captivity: "How can we sing the Lord's song in a foreign land?" The answer is two-fold. First of all, if you can't at least whisper the Lord's song under duress, then neither you nor the Lord is as substantial as one might have hoped. Secondly, it is desirable, and part of your destiny, to return to a friendlier environment where the Lord might be more fully and naturally praised .

The work of Union Station and The Depot is to return people to a warm environment where the dream of "living" might be fulfilled. Because of our work over the years, hundreds of people can say, " I have a place; I am loved; I have work to do. "This is a ministry that is worthy of whatever contribution I have made to it. It is worthy of one who is, at heart, an evangelist.

Personally, I have never had to "sing the Lord's song" out of any prolonged duress. I have almost always been in a good place in life—clothed, fed, sheltered and loved. One of the great romantic myths says that I would be a better, stronger and happier person if I could look back on some great deprivation. I disagree.

This philosophical quackery is akin to the notion that loneliness builds character, and starvation builds strong bodies. We can too easily admire the poor and leave them in their envious plight (while we strive with all our might to avoid such circumstances for ourselves and for our children).

From a safe distance we manage to miss the point that exile from the basics of life is a weakening experience. Homeless people lose their capacity to love and idle people their desire to create. Despair is irreparably debilitating. What is most devastating is that those who are able to survive the cold nights and monotonous days often retain a sense of worth only at the expense of a sense of worship.

So thank you, just the same, for not ordering my life so that it flows into or out of any great oppression. And help me through our ministry at Union Station and The Depot, through our volunteers and our staff, to restore people to a place where the essence of living—to love, to work, to worship—is available to them once again.

The Liveliness of Truth

February 11, 1988

Where does truth reside?

The government believes it is contained in laws and statistics. The church points to its creeds and doctrines. Philosophers rely on logic and scientists employ equations.

Often these kinds of truth just "sit there." Truth can be buried and dormant. It can literally "reside" in the sense that it never emerges. Just as one legitimately asks the question, "If a tree falls in an abandoned forest, does it make a sound?", one can also ponder whether truth lives up to its billing until it actually has a dynamic impact on people's lives.

Millions of Jews were imprisoned and killed under Hitler, but *The Diary of Anne Frank* brings this truth alive more than any grim statistic. Thousands of children suffered because of the Vietnam War, but the picture of a naked girl running down a street with flames leaping from her back touched the heart of a nation. The Law of Moses existed for centuries, but when Jesus fulfilled the law by healing a single man who was born blind he changed the course of civilization.

Truth waits for us to respond, to embody it and put it into action. Revelation almost always has an intimate human face to it.

I have always known, I suppose, that many of the poor of our society live unnoticed lives and die without distinction. They blend into the long gray march of humanity. But this "truth" came alive for me because of a recent personal event.

I should not have been surprised when one of our parishioners returned from delivering a Christmas poinsettia to Cleora, only to tell me that she had died a few weeks earlier. Some of us will die surrounded by family, friends, flowers and fanfare; but for others there will be no pause. The family is irretrievably scattered; the flowers are a month too late.

Yet the story of Cleora, when I think about it, does surprise me. She had a mother and father once. Several of her children survived her. (I called all the "Artzes" in the Seattle and Portland phone directories a few years ago in a vain attempt to find them.) When she was ousted from the old Taylor Hotel by a New Year's Eve fire in the mid-'70's, she got her picture in the Pasadena *Star-News*. But now there is no obituary, no remembrance.

Beyond being surprised, I am shocked and offended. God ordered creation in such a way that every human life is remarkable. At least to a mother and father. Possibly to a child. Ideally to a caring community. Everyone stands out in bold relief against the backdrop of the masses. Think of your own loved ones. Are they not precious? Is it not obscene to think of them being totally anonymous and ignored as the world passes them by? I could list 100 poor people over the years who have lived and died in utter estrangement from family, detached from the caring and creative environment that most of us enjoy. For some of these people I only know first names; for others I know life stories. Then there are those other hundreds who are so anonymous that they don't even make my list.

I remember visiting a county burial plot about ten years ago where my friend Ken Emmert was buried in a numbered grave, three deep. He was the clerk at the front desk of the same Taylor Hotel where Cleora used to live. My daughter Melissa was only a few years old then, and it took us about an hour to find the cement spike hidden beneath a tuft of grass that identified Ken's resting place. As I stood there silently, Melissa wandered off to play. She came up behind me a few minutes later with an urn filled with a beautiful fresh bouquet of flowers, and since she couldn't remember the exact location of her theft we had no choice but to leave them there for Ken. And we scampered away.

Sometimes a child will unwittingly rebel against a society which overlooks so many of its precious members. You will be relieved to know that, through years of parenting, I have managed to instill within Melissa a modicum of decency. I am optimistic that adolescence will complete her transition from the spontaneous delights of youth to the measured horrors of adulthood.

In the meantime, you will perhaps glean some truth from her childish act. And you can complete that truth by allowing it to emerge into your own life.

Remember the poor—not just by sharing your resources with them, although that is also important, but by reflecting upon their lives. I bestow some honor upon Cleora and I commend her to God simply by remembering her. There is something mystically powerful about this reflective process.

Remembering can be a life-changing experience. Truth comes into its own. I am a different person because I remember Joe pawing through trash barrels along Colorado Boulevard for food, Abe following the same route searching for coins in newspaper vending machines, Cleora musing about her lost children. These patrons of ours are dead now, but they have left a legacy. Truth emerges from their stories and enriches my life. I am a more grateful and compassionate person because of them. By remembering, I become more committed to enriching the lives of others.

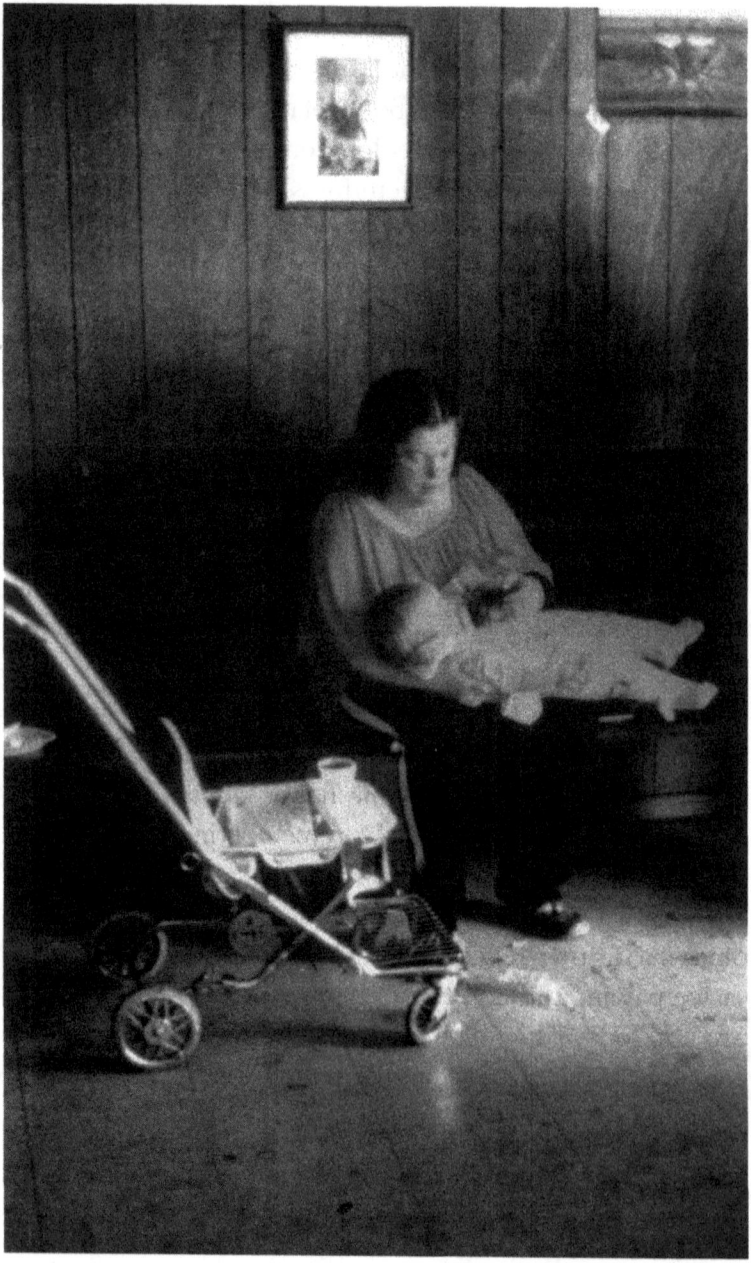

A Life That Is Fragile

March 9, 1988

A friend of mine who is a medical social worker called this morning to tell me that one of her current clients is a twelve-year-old pregnant girl. So I am led to reflect today on the sometimes overwhelming realities of life—realities I was feeling even before I heard this child's story.

Experience at Union Station and The Depot quickly teaches volunteers and staff how fragile life can be. How easy it is to upset the balance of civility in some of our relationships! How prone we are to succumb to temptation! Life seems to be a financial and ethical roller coaster.

A long time ago I learned to take advantage of the wisdom of a friend of mine who belonged to Alcoholics Anonymous. Each day is a delicate and precious gift of God. It is filled with opportunities for creativity, for love, for progress; it is also filled with options that can be devastating. Lifetime relationships can be betrayed; years of sobriety can be aborted. And many other realities could befall us that are completely outside of our control.

How do we respond to life that is so fragile?

First of all I believe we respond with gratitude for the joys and blessings that are ours. We celebrate the moment and then place it in our memories where it may enrich us for years to come.

Secondly, we respond with sympathy for those who have

not survived so well in this survival-of-the-fittest world. Never look down upon those who are life's casualties. We have construed life to be a contest with winners and losers, so we should not be surprised or offended that "losers" are strewn about the landscape of our relationships and experiences.

Thirdly, become involved in the world of the "non-survivors." It may already be a familiar world to you, or it may soon become familiar. I doubt if any of us can escape it altogether. But the point here is to venture into this world voluntarily with an eye to self-improvement and renewed commitment. I learn a great deal about myself and my upward and downward mobility when I work in the Union Station/Depot environment.

Fourthly, treat the non-survivors in your company as an opportunity to share, to creatively and constructively help. Pass by the opportunity to gloat, to feel self-righteous and pretend that God or fate was recognizing your merits when talent, blessing and good fortune were distributed.

Finally, trust that the inherent goodness of creation will finally overcome the overwhelming disabilities and injuries of life. And more importantly, know that this resource of goodness can bring hope and change today to your own brokenness and to those whom you love. The human condition is always subject to change.

Unlike fate or luck, this resource of goodness is accessible to us. I am exhilarated by the realizable potential for food and shelter, for health care and rehabilitation, for decent housing and meaningful work and the healing of relationships. These are not distant or aloof possibilities. If there is a God, then goodness is within our grasp.

So the overwhelming despair of some circumstances can never be elevated to a dominant status. Hope is the ultimate context for living. The data of life that bombards and depresses us can be transformed into our own renewed dedication. Through our program at Union Station and The Depot, we have seen that dedication on the part of our staff and volunteers and donors produces tangible results.

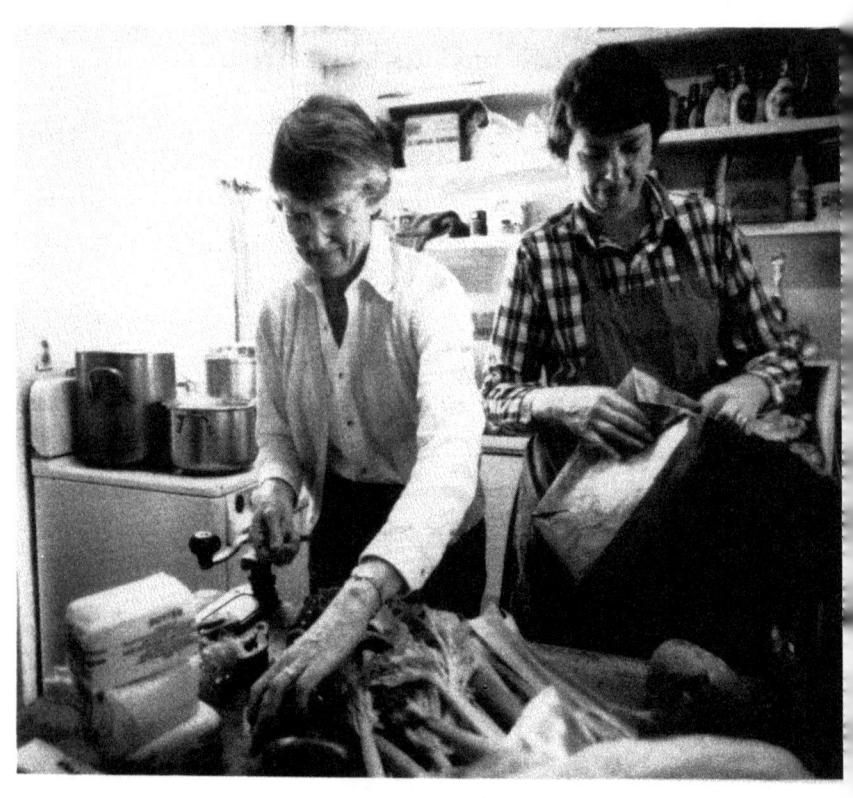

Addiction to Duty

April 13, 1988

If you began each day by asking, "Where is joy for me today? Where can I find some adventure?", what would your answer be?

Many of us do in fact begin the day with this question implicitly or explicitly guiding us in our choices. Society as a whole has traveled many paths marked "joy" and "adventure" and "euphoria" only to be disappointed. I am going to suggest a path too often overlooked.

Frank Cook was one of our stalwart Union Station volunteers until he died several years ago. He was a retired butler to English admiralty, and he brought to his tasks at the Station the same fastidious attention to detail and devotion to cleanliness that had made him so suited to his profession. But he was an anomaly at the Station because he expected our patrons to adhere to standards of discipline that many had abandoned long ago.

So after hours, when Frank could frequently be found mopping the floor or cleaning the refrigerator, he would bend my ear a bit. "Bill, you should have seen the amount of sugar that Joe poured in his coffee today. Why does Mary drink so much? George is young and strong and could get a job if he only tried."

But Frank wouldn't miss a beat in his cleaning routine while he complained about various people, and sometimes it seemed that on the surface, at least, he didn't like very much the ones he was voluntarily serving with such diligence. So I asked Frank one day (and then many days thereafter in what became a ritual conversation):

"Why do you devote yourself to serving the poor who so often disappoint you? Surely there are other corners of the world that need cleaning, and where you might find more gratification."

And Frank's smile would broaden to fill the room. His eyes would twinkle as we went through this dialogue. And he would tell me for the hundredth time, "Because, Bill, it is my duty."

Frank was a too rare individual who took great delight in doing his duty. He thrived on it. The path marked "duty" is a road "less travelled by" that can make all the difference, to recall Robert Frost's wonderful poem. Frank discovered this path and it gave to his life beauty and nobility.

Try an experiment with me for a week. When you arise in the morning, ask yourself, "What is my duty today?" Then do your best to allow room for duty on your crowded schedule.

Of course, you will be helped to make this experiment succeed if you rediscover with me some of life's basic duties. These can be an unexpected source of joy and meaning. I am not referring to the standard duties of going to the office or doing homework or mowing the lawn.

Normally, when we feel depressed or overwhelmed we look to some of society's favorite antidotes. We need a "fix"—some escape of food or drugs or entertainment or fantasy. But duty itself can be a "fix." You can actually indulge yourself by undertaking some tasks that you heretofore thought were draining rather than uplifting.

You can "escape" by returning to the ancient admonitions that now, rather than simply arousing your conscience, can satisfy your appetite for adventure. What are these basic ennobling duties?

Care for the poor. Visit the sick. Help the less fortunate.

"That's it?" you say in disbelief. "My life is falling apart. I need a vacation. The highlight of my year so far has been watching television. And you want me to escape these realities by giving a sandwich to someone who is hungry, by staying overnight at The Depot? You must be desperate for volunteers!"

Actually, we are not desperate for volunteers. You're the one who is desperate. And you may continue to lead a relatively empty life until you rediscover that adventure lies in duty and duty lies in serving others—tangibly reaching out to someone in need.

I am not talking about achieving some uplift as a result of seeing the misery of others. I can find at Union Station and The Depot a renewed sense of gratitude for life's blessings, but that is not the issue here. The secret is that duty contains within itself a life-giving elixir—so powerful that one can become addicted to it. I have come to understand that Frank Cook was addicted to mopping the floor at Union Station.

The Jewish Bible holds out the promise that one can thrive upon righteousness. Society doesn't pay much heed. We want results, even in the social service industry. All of our staff and volunteers are gratified when they see changed lives. But Frank was the epitomy of the volunteer whose eyes could not contain the twinkle that arose from simply doing his duty, no matter what the results.

Define this duty to others as best you can in concrete and

personalized ways. Instead of filling your day only with those obligations that society or your job imposes upon you, carve out some opportunity to tangibly serve the poor. Reach out to someone who can use your help. Find your own ways to test the theory. This basic duty to others can be more than an add-on to life, it can be the essence. Duty can become a new and helpful affection, expelling a lot of old and unhelpful ones. And, like all true affections, it can impart to you a sense of joy and adventure.

Seeking Christ in Others

August 8, 1988

One of the refrains I hear each week in worship is a statement of a noble goal:

"To seek and serve Christ in all persons."

The idea of "serving Christ" in other people—encountering the face of Christ in the faces of the poor—is familiar to me. This powerful concept lies behind the whole idea of Union Station. When we give a bowl of soup or a shelter bed to someone who is hungry or homeless, we are giving it to Christ, the Gospels tell us.

No matter what your religious beliefs, or lack of same, there is room for you in the small kitchen at Union Station. But somewhere in your consciousness, cloaked in some ideology or theology that is comfortable to you, I suspect you will find a variation on this scriptural theme: "When you do it to the least of these, you do it unto me."

So this concept of "serving" Christ in others is familiar to me, but what about this idea of "seeking" Christ in other people? What does this mean?

As our staff comes in contact with the masses of the poor and homeless during the course of a year at Union Station and The Depot, we hear hundreds of stories and become involved to some degree in hundreds of lives. To "seek" Christ in these people, I believe, is to seek that responsiveness in them that brings together their most human and most divine traits.

The human impulse is to survive and succeed, yet John, a composite of some of our patrons, doesn't seem to care about survival or success.

The motivational factors that we take for granted have been eroded by years of failure. So when you hold out to John what you take to be a glorious opportunity, perhaps even a chance to escape the cycle of poverty, the response is bewildering. Sometimes I'm tempted to literally shake some of our patrons into reality and ask them, "What's wrong with you? Here's a chance to change your situation, and you're letting it slip away!"

Again, we are often confronted by people who seem to be totally devoid of "divine" traits. The divine impulse is to love and to serve. How do we account then for some of the callousness and cruelty that so many evidence among us? The human-divine "Christ" that is within each of us must be allowed to breathe and flourish. This is a dynamic and invigorating "Christ,"—this urge to survive and succeed, to love and serve. This is an instinct meant to shape our lives, but sometimes it is buried beneath numerous perverse instincts that lead us way off course. Surviving and succeeding deteriorate into conquering and oppressing. Loving and serving become a condescending manipulation of the lives and hopes of others. Loneliness and hostility set in.

We must strive, I believe, to seek the "Christ" in others—their true human and divine nature—and not be put off by perversity. So we love our enemies; we seek the "Christ" in them, not according to what we perceive to be their worthiness. We have more faith in the "Christ" in others than we do in their more visible waywardness. You can't really succeed in the long run at Union Station/The Depot if you don't seek the

"Christ" in others.

To be honest, sometimes people leave us shaking our heads and muttering to ourselves in disbelief, "I'd sure like to find the Christ in that person!" But if there is no "Christ" in that person, our ministry is in vain, so we can't afford to give too much credibility to our doubts. We've got to keep our doubts in the "doubt" category and our beliefs in the "belief" category.

A real patron (not a composite!) reported to me this week how his life had finally gotten into forward gear after several years of running in reverse. Many people had given up on him and his future. But some persevered enough to seek and find the "Christ" in him, and their patience has now been rewarded. So I said to my friend, "What made the difference?" And he responded, "I got tired of being unhappy."

Aha! There's the "Christ" emerging. Christ draws us toward happiness and fulfillment, and this instinctive quest is what needs to be reawakened in the lives of many (including some of us).

This inner Christ, the urge to survive and succeed, to love and serve, is present, at least in disguise, in all people. We have to keep seeking. And when we've given up on ourselves or on others and come to the conclusion that there is no resident Christ to be found, we have to start our search anew.

Why such persistence? Because the health and power of the "Christ" within me is dependent on my bond with the "Christ" in others. I can stop seeking about as easily as I can stop breathing.

Charity Is Who You Are

September 14, 1988

The cover of the September 5 issue of *Time Magazine* repeats the question I am most often asked: "Begging in America—To Give or Not to Give?"

"Should I give to panhandlers?" If I had a quarter for every time I have been asked that question, I would have a quarter for every one who has ever asked me for a quarter!

The article in *Time* offers some good insights. It talks about the fear and guilt that often taint these curbside transactions, the element of conning on the part of many and of genuine desperation on the part of some. It alludes to the fact that there are more responsible ways to contribute money and services to the poor than by hastily donating a few coins, preserving one's anonymity and detachment in the process. The article reminds me of the fact that there is a latent hostility toward the homeless and the dependent that is fostered by a society that prides itself in its perceived "rugged individualism." This conflicting data does not give us a definitive answer as to what we should do.

What the article does not include is a clear articulation of the major reason I am reluctant to give to panhandlers. The noble concept of charity suffers a horrible fate in the process.

How do you view charity? Is it the weak response of the fearful and guilty? Is it peripheral to the real dynamic thrust of your life? Is it strictly a monetary or checkbook transaction?

Charity can be a consuming passion, a rich and invigorating opportunity. To the extent that it becomes your "reason for being," you will be among the most fulfilled people in the world. Charity is the greatest of the triumvirate of uniquely human virtues—faith, hope and charity—not so much because of what it demands of you but because of what it contributes to you.

Permit me to cite a more personal example. My mother, now 73, is the personification of this ethic of charity. She is not a heroine or a saint of the pedestal variety, not a "Mother-Teresa," and I don't want to hold up her life as some unreachable or unique model of unparalleled virtue. (Sorry, Mom!) Yet Miriam Lane has spent most of her adult life as a registered nurse, and most of her professional life working with handicapped children. She retired many years ago, but she still spends much of her time as a "best friend" to people who are at John J. Kane Hospital, south of Pittsburgh. This is charity, and my mother is the richer for it, as much as society is. This is what keeps my mother going in addition to her continuing attempts to raise her three middle-aged children. Along with one of her like-minded friends, she has started recently a friendship and visitation group for seniors at her church. Her charity will always find a way to express itself. Charity is in her bones .

This kind of quality giving of one's time, this investment of emotion and energy, is what charity is all about. I'm not sure that giving to panhandlers on the street is even on the same continuum, and it is certainly not a substitute. There is no passion to it, no creativity, and very little rehabilitation or redemption, for either the donor or the donee.

I think I see one other aspect of my mother's brand of charity that is helpful to me. Charity is not so much something my mother does as who she is. It transcends the realm of politics and ideology and reason. At its best, charity is a response to the goodness of life—to God, to nature, to the abiding quality of mercy that accompanies every waking day.

So we are to "walk in love"—making our way through life by availing ourselves of those natural, unforced occasions to be charitable.

As children of God, charity is our most basic instinct. As citizens or our world, it is our compelling opportunity.

The Sacred Chair

October 12, 1988

Today I want to tell you the story (slightly embellished!) of the sacred chair.

I worship each week in a church which takes great care in its presentation of the weekly liturgy. During the Sunday morning service, everything is in its place and the opening sentences, prayers, anthems, scriptures, sermon and offertory flow smoothly. There is a pervading sense of security and rightness to all that transpires.

And not by accident! Every week the staff spends time together ironing out the details, and then reviewing each service after the fact.

On Sunday I always sit in the same pew, just in front of the Children's Altar, and one morning several years ago an old wooden chair appeared, placed neatly beside the altar, and every time I lifted my eyes and faced front I looked squarely at that chair.

It was rather ugly and beaten, totally devoid of any compelling outward beauty. Yet I knew there was a deeper significance to that chair, placed as it was so prominently and precisely, for all to see. Perhaps it was an original piece of furniture from some noteworthy setting; perhaps a Bishop had sat in it!

During the service I always promised myself that I would inquire as to the chair's history, but I became so enraptured Sunday after Sunday that I would never remember after the service was over, until the next occasion for worship, when whispered inquiry was strictly forbidden.

Then one Sunday the chair disappeared. I was never quite so disoriented during worship as I was that week. After the service, thinking that this noble specimen of ancient craftsmanship had been sent to the shop for polishing or repair, I accosted the verger, who is, in the Episcopal tradition, the source of authority for such matters.

"Oh, that old thing," he said. "It was such an eyesore that we threw it in the dumpster."

And not a moment too soon, I exclaimed to myself, after having been affronted by that sad example of obsolescence for far too long.

It is amazing, isn't it, how we can give credibility to some realities, after we have coexisted with them for some time, even though they are inherently outrageous. The human spirit has a tremendous ability to adjust to the status quo, without ever having the opportunity to knowingly participate in its establishment. Sometimes we are poorly served by this ability.

What "sacred chairs" are staring us in the face today that really have no place in our society?

Did we ever really vote to live in a world under threat of nuclear annihilation? Did we choose to make our home in a prosperous society where the needs of several million of our fellow citizens for food and housing are addressed at a snail's pace?

Frequently I drive through northwest Pasadena, where thousands of people, mostly ethnic minorities, are crammed into housing that is often substandard. But I don't think "racism;" I just accept. And when I visit Skid Row, Los Angeles, where at night I see thousands make their beds out of pavement and newspapers, the affront is transformed into apathetic acceptance.

That's the way things are. And some elusive self-ordained authority has set the stage wisely and deliberately, while by default I fall into the passive role of silent assent.

Inquiring minds want to know, and devout spirits want to mobilize to change reality, wherever the affront can be exposed for what it is. This role as change agents working in a setting that is not as sacred as we imagine it to be is the role of children of God. We think that social change is a very complex matter, and that we are not up to the task. I am convinced, though, that all of the obstacles can be overcome with relative ease—given the fact that we are a creative and energetic people at our best—if only someone has the courage to ask the right question.

So the starting point is, "Why do we have to put up with that ugly chair?" Begin each day with that question, and you will be surprised at how many changes, small and large, can make life more beautiful and human.

The Seductions of Sharing

Thanksgiving, 1988

Dean Alan Jones of Grace Cathedral in San Francisco tells a story that is appropriate for us as we enter this holiday season. It is the story of a rabbi who asks his students about the dawning of true light.

"When can you tell that day is breaking?"

One student suggests that it is when there is enough light to distinguish between a fox and a dog on the road. "No," insists the rabbi, "that's not the right answer."

Another student ventures to answer the question. "It's when you look at an orchard and you can tell the difference between an apple and a pear tree."

The rabbi shakes his head and the students, in frustration, all shout, "Then tell us, when can you tell when the day has dawned?"

The rabbi replies, "Day breaks when you look at a man or a woman and know that he or she is your brother or your sister. Until you can do that, no matter what time of day it is, it is always night."

So it is at Union Station and The Depot, our hospitality center and shelter for Pasadena's hungry and homeless. The most basic statement of why we have been in the business of helping people since 1973 is captured in this story. We are responding, without any agenda of imposed judgment or ideology, to the needs of our sisters and brothers.

One of the things I have discovered about my own life is how puny it is and how inconsequential it may be. I only take up a little space on the planet (although a bit more than I should!), and I am only worth a brief mention in the exhaustive diary of human history. Yet my life is transformed into a glorious presence when I enter the arena of sharing with others.

Last Saturday I visited with a widow who, with her late husband, came into Union Station regularly when we were located on Union Street in Old Town. Today she is in a nursing home, in relative good health and good spirits. I hope I brought her some encouragement on Saturday. But the point is, the opportunity to share some time with her—to boldly enter the arena where some of my "sisters and brothers, mothers and fathers" live in loneliness and discouragement—is an opportunity to enrich my own life. I just can't get over the purity of the high that comes with grassroots giving. By receiving my friendship, she lends to my life a nobility that makes me feel like a king.

As I left her room, I looked in the hallway mirror to see if a crown had magically appeared on my head, as in the old Imperial margarine commercials.

But a word of warning is in order. Be careful as you share your time and money with the less fortunate this holiday season, especially if you do it in a personal way. The potent seductiveness of sharing is a powerful force, and I know many who have fallen prey to its addictive nature.

Occasional acts of goodness can lead to vocational and lifestyle changes, perhaps years later. Of course, this is just the medicine that some of us need to rescue our flagging fortunes, as we feel our lives plummeting into obscurity and meaninglessness.

There is something about the discerning of family, about brothers and sisters in need, that overwhelms one with a basic sense of rightness. This is the real stuff of life, and I commend it to you. This is the dawning of the day.

The Miseries of Christmas Eve

January 11, 1989

What do a Wiseman, a Santa Claus and a Mr. Fix-It have in common?

They are the three roles I assumed on Christmas Eve in an attempt to carry out my varied responsibilities. I am reminded of a story I once heard about General Douglas MacArthur.

He was asked what he would list as the three most important hallmarks of a good soldier. He answered: "Duty, duty, duty."

Sometimes it's helpful to me, as I deal with a frustrating jumble of needs and opportunities, to remember the simplicity of that approach. What is the most useful thing for me to be doing right now with my time? Without worrying too much about the meaning of life, about tomorrow, about all the problems I have failed to solve or even address, what presents itself to me as my most immediate duty? If I can answer that question, then proceed accordingly, I find that life takes on a certain enriching orderliness. And the transcendent questions about meaning and fulfillment tend to take care of themselves.

I admit that this can be a dangerous approach, because in the name of duty people go marching in all different directions, sometimes for good and sometimes for evil. First you must adopt a system of values—a religious conviction—that people are created in the image of God, that life and creation belong to God, and that to share the goodness of life and creation with others is your human destiny. Now you are ready to do your duty.

So let's return to Christmas Eve. Just as I was about to participate in a Christmas drama at a four o'clock family church service with a brief appearance as a wiseman visiting Bethlehem, I was handed a note that told me that a crisis was developing at the hotels on Los Angeles' Skid Row because the Christmas Eve downpour was flooding out some of our tenants. I am involved with a project to renovate three dilapidated structures on Main Street and to manage them as single-room-occupancy hotels for poor people. Earlier on Christmas Eve I had arranged for the delivery of beautiful Christmas baskets to the 17 residential tenants who were living there during the extensive renovation period—which included putting on a new roof. I was already worried about the rain ruining our Christmas Day Dinner-in-the-Park. Now it appeared to be ruining Christmas Eve as well, so in between church services I dispatched a colleague with a huge roll of plastic to see if a few holes could be temporarily patched.

I also wanted him to tell the tenants not to expect an overnight miracle, in view of the continuing rain and the fact that the roof had gaping holes in it, but Christmas Eve is the precise time in history for overnight miracles. The entire day I seemed to be out of sync with God's purposes. You know the feeling.

In between church services I also delivered some Christmas gifts to a few elderly Union Station patrons who were shut-ins and alone, getting soaking wet in the process because I had tucked my newly-acquired umbrella neatly under something, somewhere. I remember muttering to myself that this was the worst Christmas Eve I had ever spent.

My duty also required that I pay a brief visit at 9 p.m. to our 15 overnight guests at The Depot, people who would be homeless if it were not for Union Station's efforts. But I still experienced little in the way of gratification. I was too wet, too tired and too fearful for the Christmas weather outlook. If I couldn't be happy, I wanted to make a few other people happy. I wanted to do my duty.

Now I am sure you suppose that somewhere in this long ordeal, lasting until 1 o'clock Christmas morning, a smile returned to my face and a warm glow once again filled my being. Not so. I went to bed demoralized, and I would still call this my worst Christmas Eve ever. Hopefully my despondency did not seep through to the people I was trying to cheer, to the children who viewed my wiseman portrayal.

The moral of the story is not that everything quickly rights itself in life if we can only persevere for a few hours. Even if Christmas Day did turn out bright and crisp, I am not so sure someone still doesn't owe me an explanation for the miseries of Christmas Eve.

The moral of the story is duty, duty, duty. Somewhere in my youth I must have been taught that when life becomes overwhelming, the most important response is carrying out one's immediate obligations.

Life for us in 1989 may be more overwhelming, and we will need to sustain our dutiful response. Whether we are rich or poor, healthy or disabled, sane or addicted, life contains an element of ordeal. While I do not subscribe to the "warm glow" school of thought that says that good feelings quickly follow every good deed, I do believe that duty breeds an abiding joy.

The Mysteries of Christmas Day

Christmas, 1988

Everybody loves a good mystery. We love to see it unfold before us, and we are amazed at how all the questions and paradoxes are gathered together at the climax so that firmness and clarity once again assert themselves.

But we hate to be a participant in a mystery that is still in process, whose conclusion is still the object of our anxiety.

Yet so it is with life that flows out of the Christmas Story—the mystery of how a God so transcendent could become engaged in our lives with such intimacy and openness. We love to observe mystery but we are not so eager to participate. So we come to the manger in awe, with our gifts and adoration, but we too often leave the presence of God's love, ourselves unchanged.

God's love for the world, when we meditate upon it, represents such a profound mystery to us: power is made weak; the eternal becomes specific to a time and place; the invincible reaches out in vulnerable expression.

This is the mystery of who God is, and it is so inviting to us, yet so filled with the terror of the unknown. We are secure in our own niche in life, aloof from all the brokenness that fills our world. We are touched by the failure and sadness that our own lives have brought to us just enough to know that we want to escape any semblance of inadequacy. If God is eager to be a child among us, to grow up in a world of temptation and confusion, to become the hapless servant of the sick and the lonely, then we are just as eager to escape those same realities.

Christmas is synonymous with mystery. It is a night filled with the terror of a truth that cannot be grasped in its entirety. In our haste to be strong we pass along the way a God whose opposite journey is in the direction of weakness. And all the accumulated self-confidence of a life of accomplishment dissolves before the mystery of the manger. How long it has taken us to arrive at self-assuredness! Yet how quickly all of our pretense is reduced to weeping.

Oh how we hate this ambiguity. If God would just hold out to us in a clear and compelling way exactly what life is. We only want to do what is right and to follow the Star.

To those who share my religious tradition, Christmas is the stream of love and goodness that feeds our existence and that brings us to the very edge of glory. We can reach out and touch truth at Christmas just as certainly as Mary caressed her newborn child. We are invited by this child to abandon our security and composure and to enter a world that jostles us with its demands and that challenges all of our assumptions. We will have to find a faith that is greater than we ever contemplated.

No matter what your own tradition, I believe that faith in a God who gives away God's life to the world can be a transforming faith for you. I myself have followed this approximate path—this journey of compassion—for many years. My pace has been so leisurely that I will never experience all of the truth that God originally intended for me. Yet I have looked out upon vistas of truth that are incomparable in their glory. I mistake each one for my final destination so that I am reluctant to move on in response to God's new challenges. There is still so much mystery here that I am alternately dissuaded by fear of the unknown and seduced by the glory of the Christmas Story.

I know what my life needs. It needs that glory of God that we celebrate at Christmas, that leads us to caress a broken world. May the glory of this season come home to us and satisfy all of our yearnings. And may we trust God's truth enough to participate in that mystery that can yet transform our lives and our civilization.

The Poor and the Potential for Greatness

February, 1989

One of my favorite Peanuts cartoons features Linus emoting endlessly about his own potential for greatness. He looks in awe at his hands as he stretches them skyward. And he concludes: "These are hands which may someday accomplish great things... These are hands which may do marvelous works! They may build mighty bridges, or heal the sick, or hit home-runs, or write soul-stirring novels! These are hands which may someday change the course of destiny!"

He is so enthralled with the prospects for his own immortality that he falls to notice Lucy standing by his side, totally unimpressed with his analysis. She glances at Linus' hands and succinctly points out: "They've got jelly on them!"

Whereupon Linus lowers his head and drifts quietly out of the picture, abandoning all his pretensions.

Too bad that Lucy was able to bluff Linus out of his flirtation with greatness. Lucy is of the mistaken opinion that goodness and greatness emerge from pure motivations and clean hands. Yet at the very foundation of every human achievement there is some crippling reality, some debilitating flaw. And pretense is the temporary scaffolding that enables us to pursue some righteous endeavor, despite our handicaps, and to establish some reality that will last after the pretense vanishes.

The words that are laden with hope for our age are the words: "Let's pretend." Those of us who are adults disparage the notion as if it were unworthy of mature thought. Yet progress can evolve if we allow ourselves to flirt with the following pretensions:

"Let's pretend that every child in America had a home."

"Let's pretend that every able adult had meaningful work to do."

"Let's pretend that everyone sick or disabled had access to health care."

"Let's pretend that all of our citizens could learn how to read and write."

"Let's pretend that no one had to live continually with the pangs of hunger."

"Let's pretend that the mistrust and alienation that needlessly perpetuate loneliness could be overcome."

"Let's pretend that those suffering from addiction could find a place in a residential treatment facility without a six-month wait."

You may say that it is wrong for me, even dangerous, to live with such fantasies. Yet it may be even more dangerous to live with their opposite realities. Fantasy can be the pathway for hope and progress, while those who occupy themselves too much with reality can become the apostles of stagnation and despair.

So it's too bad that the Lucys of the world so easily rob us of our dreams. Of course we are limited and fallible. Our hands have jelly on them. And yet...

...our progress at Union Station over the years in solving the difficult human dilemmas that thousands of poor people have brought to us has been inspiring.

...our growth as an organization has been an uplifting chronicle of meaningful expansion.

Yet for all of those years, since 1973, our "hands" have (quite literally) had jelly on them. Our motivations are impure. Our volunteers are subject to burnout. Our policies are flawed. Our compassion is unevenly administered. Our programs are sometimes self-serving.

We know that dreaming endlessly about how things could be better is not sufficient. We need to act upon our dreams. But that is not as difficult a barrier to overcome as the barrier that exists with someone who has given up dreaming altogether. In fact, the most difficult situation we face at Union Station and The Depot is resignation to the status quo.

Some people have been separated from their dreams by so many failures over such a long period of time, that to ask them to think of themselves in a better life situation is impossible. They have given up all their pretenses and have accommodated themselves to the despair of the moment. They don't allow themselves to think of what their lives might be. And the greatest tragedy—the greatest humiliation—is that they don't think of themselves as having anything to share with the rest of us.

When you work with the poor, it's best to think of each one as someone with an incredible gift locked up inside, a gift to share with the rest of humanity. Each homeless woman carries with her a greatness; each unemployed man a precious contribution; each hungry child a potential to change the course of civilization.

So God has given us a great trust—to care for the poor. The most important part of our caring is to elicit from each one, no matter what the outward circumstances, that inward unique beauty that earmarks all of us as children of God. Linus was right to see the outline of immortality within his human grasp.

Our hope this day is that we can sense that greatness in our own potential, no matter what limitations we must overcome, and that we can also accord to others these divine possibilities.

Finding the Shape of God

March 1, 1989

One of the beliefs that has sustained me in my ministry is the belief that there are no problems without solutions. My experience tells me there are such problems—in my own life, in the lives of those I touch, in the corporate and global fabric of our world. But my faith in God and in the inherent goodness of creation gives me the more optimistic and overriding viewpoint.

The people who believe that society is beset by insoluble dilemmas—crime, drugs, mental illness, homelessness, hunger, ignorance, racism—consign too many situations too quickly to that category of despair. But if we give in to depression, we're not much good to anybody.

As a boy, I occasionally went fishing, although I never became much of a sportsman. In fact, my career as a fisherman is a pretty depressing saga. Today I am angling and casting about in different ways, but there is a subtle relationship, because as a boy I transformed my frustration into gratification.

I spent most of my time fishing unraveling my line. The ratio of time spent unraveling to actually fishing was astronomically disproportionate. I caught perhaps eight fish in my entire life as a sportsman. On the other hand, as an unraveler, the accomplishments were endless.

Now here's the strange thing. After a while I began to

receive more gratification from unraveling my line than from catching fish. I might have come skipping home joyously on a sunny afternoon to be greeted by my parents with the question, "Did you catch anything?" "No, but I got my line unraveled! "

This was God and nature's way of preserving my boyhood enthusiasm. I believed then, and I believe with all my heart now, that if a line gets raveled, it can get unraveled; if there's a way into the woods, there's a way home again.

This belief has served me well, and it has a lot to do with my belief in God. Belief in God is the anchor around which hopefulness coalesces into action. Compassion and duty, justice and mercy all emerge from a belief that creation at its very core is God's creation. And it is therefore wholesome. And no situation or human being, no matter how degraded, is beyond reach. The core of goodness is still there.

Unraveling is a matter of working one's way back to the core, so that life can flow once again the way God intended.

If you get frustrated and concede defeat about life, remember the story of Noah's Ark—the time in history when God gave up on goodness. God decided to cut the knot and start over. But God repented of that approach, and the rainbow is the sign of God's covenant with us that never again will the possibilities of redemption be taken too lightly.

There is enough room in the world to house every human being. There is enough water to satisfy thirst. There is enough meaningful work to fulfill the yearning for creative expression. There is a wide enough embrace to encompass our whole human family in the arms of God.

The thrill of my work at Union Station and The Depot is the thrill of unraveling problems, of getting to the core, of recreating opportunities, of seeing life blossom and flow. The thrill doesn't come every day. Some of the knots people bring us are so complex that we want to throw up our hands. And sometimes we do.

But I will never say that the problems are too large. I will only say that on a given day, the solutions I can bring are too small. That fine distinction may be no comfort to the person who is lonely, confused, despairing. But I have to take care of my own spirit, dissipate my own loneliness and limit my own confusion. The hope I can carry into tomorrow's entanglements is the one indispensable ingredient.

Some of us, whether we are rich or poor, look within ourselves and see a shambles of lost ambition and wasted opportunity. I see that gloomy picture in myself some of the time, and I see it in many of the people who come to me for help. Where is the goodness?

Remember those labyrinthine puzzles you were given as a child? From one angle they were a meaningless maze, but from another angle there was the shape of a bird or a dog or a flower. I think of some of the people who have come over the years: Jesse, Jimmy, Freddie and Janey, Linden, hundreds of others. As they revealed to me the disarray of their lives, I always found the shape of God in the midst.

Find the shape of God, in yourself or in another, and life will take on a loveliness, a hopefulness, an expression of mercy.

Our Silent Successes

April 5, 1989

Fourteen years ago there was a man whom I will call James (for the purposes of this letter) who came to Union Station when it was located at its original Union Street site in Old Town Pasadena. I remember James clearly, although I didn't know him too well, and I hadn't seen him since those early days.

So imagine my shock when I walked into Union Station at Walnut and Euclid recently to see James giving his testimony to a group of 12- Steppers, our daily program akin to Alcoholics Anonymous for those recovering from addiction. James has been sober for many years now, and he obviously enjoyed returning to help the people and the organization that had helped him so much back in 1975.

I spoke at a luncheon recently, and during the question and answer period Union Station was politely criticized for not being too successful with a group of street people who were hanging out daily, and with some negative social implications, at a Pasadena street corner. I knew the group, some of whom came to the Station for food and some of whom did not, and decided to plead guilty to the charge of ineffectiveness but, as the court would say, "with an explanation."

The explanation centers around the fact that our human failures at Union Station are apparent, but our successes are not. Unlike James, people who are helped by our staff and volunteers seldom come back to return the favor. They "graduate" from the Station or The Depot, and they close a chapter in their lives that has caused them great pain, a chapter they don't want to remember.

If a person does battle with alcoholism, drug abuse, hunger, homelessness, unemployment, or mental illness, and that person survives, many scars are left. No one escapes the ravages of life on the streets unscathed. And most want to forget these darkest days of their lives.

Life is very fragile, not just for the people who drop occasionally into the "down and out" categories, but for all of us. The pitfalls are numerous, and they almost literally reach out to devour us if we get too close. So, understandably, we don't have a very active "Union Station/Depot Alumni Association." People who escape the devouring social demons don't want to relive their nightmares.

But hundreds of people have escaped, through the encouragement of our little band of helpers who dish out food and friendship and shelter beds. I hear from some occasionally. They also congregate at street corners with their colleagues, but they don't wear a button that says, "I'm a former street person."

So you have to judge us by our silent successes, not just by our glaring failures, when it comes to counting up the lives of those with restored futures and renewed hopes. And only God can make that count.

The second part of my "guilty, with an explanation" statement is that our work is extremely difficult. The people who come to our doorstep have usually exhausted every relationship and every resource that might help them. We are their last resort. And their problems have gotten worse as they have sifted their way downward through family and friends, jobs and savings accounts and health. There is a great stigma attached to life on the streets in our society, and this subculture of despair and destitution is resisted until the sheer weight of reality forces the issue.

So our staff is challenged daily to use great care and ingenuity. Warm smiles don't solve too many of the problems, although we start with a smile and simple listening skills. When we are successful in resurrecting a human life, sometimes we are more surprised than the beneficiary of our compassion! "How did that happen," we murmur to ourselves, when a successful scenario unfolds before us.

So I say to James, who is so grateful for what we did for him, "Tell me what we did, so we can do it also for Mary and John and Frank and Earl." But there is no "formula" for success, and our staff and volunteers are not assembly line workers putting together people's lives according to some diagram. Our work is much more creative and spiritual than we know how to explain.

Be patient with us...those of you who support us and those of you who benefit from our services. We are doing our best in the midst of the most difficult human circumstances.

The Aspirations of the Poor

June 5, 1989

I recently came across a poem written about 400 years ago by an Englishman named Sir Edward Dyer. The first stanza of "The Lowest Trees Have Topps" contains a thought that has often crossed my mind in my work with the poor, yet I could never express it so beautifully:

> The lowest trees have topps, the ante her gall,
> The flie her spleene, the little sparke his heat:
> The slender hairs cast shadows, though but small,
> And bees have stinges, although they be not great;
> Seas have their sourse, and soe have shallow springes:
> And Love is Love, in beggers and in Kinges.

As frequently as I find myself at home among the poor, I also move among the rich and the privileged of our society. Dyer writes correctly that "Love is Love, in beggers and in Kinges."

When I stand in the back of the room to observe one of our 12-Step meetings at Union Station, I hear the addicted and the homeless speak of their aspirations. I see meaningful relationships develop among the people of Skid Row. The daily life of a child is filled, just as mine is, with a mixture of fear and hope.

One of the most compelling arguments for the idea that

we all are rooted in the spirit of a Creator-God is the fact that we all possess a reservoir of aspiration, a potential for love, a uniquely human quest for meaning that characterizes both the rich and the poor among us.

One of the poorest men I ever knew spoke with me one day about his life. He possessed only the clothes on his back. His memory was so dimmed by disability that he could not remember the names of his distant children. And he confessed to me: "The only thing I have to hold on to is my faith in God."

The second stanza of Dyer's poem contains this appropriate commentary: "The firmest fayth is fownd in fewest woordes."

But the point I want to make now, in this letter, is that the reason we are persisting in such a concerted way with our ministry to our patrons is because "the lowest trees have topps!"

Why devote so much of our lives and fortunes to the least of our brothers and sisters? Why have such an emphasis on volunteer labor? Why employ such a competent and committed staff? I believe we have the finest and most dedicated people working for us as there are in any social service ministry anywhere.

Our standards of commitment and excellence in ministry are so high because we are dealing with a precious commodity: the aspirations of the poor! In a society that acts sometimes as if some people are expendable—the elderly, the low-skilled, the mentally ill, the addicted—we nurture the notion that all of these friends have "topps." They reach out, perhaps in a very fragile and tentative way, for a place, a home, work to do, meaning in life.

Our ministry is dedicated to these people who cast only a slender shadow across the landscape of civilization. Our new facility will be dedicated to them, as are all the daily efforts and the financial support that produce a couple hundred meals at breakfast and lunch, 20 shelter beds each night, and a host of other services.

The aspirations I observe in people are often in miniature form. People learn to lower their sights in the face of frustration, hostility, and a lack of prior success. Self-esteem is diminished, especially among the least "fit" in a society that prides itself in the "survival of the fittest."

People around the world who can't have freedom adjust to a miniaturized version. People who will never be healthy again hope for a modicum of comfort. Those who will always be poor can find hope in cardboard boxes for homes and bread for food. The dynamic of aspiration is still the same, although the objective is more bite-sized. But the important reality is that the aspiration of the human spirit is never extinguished.

And another important reality that we deal with each day is that the downward trend of self-esteem can be reversed. Success builds on success. So the addicted person who has a fleeting desire for only one day of sobriety can travel that upward path to greater confidence. The person who enjoys a first hot meal at Union Station can gain a renewed appetite for substantial nourishment. People can learn to work again, to enjoy life, to fall in love. Not in a day, but in a progression of days.

So this is why we keep at it. We believe that even "the lowest trees have topps."

A Journey to Skid Row

(Excerpts from a speech given on behalf of the Church & Temple Housing Corporation at the Rector's Forum, All Saints Church, on April 2, 1989.)

The project of buying and renovating three Skid Row hotels, and of moving to Skid Row to oversee the effort, brings a different world, almost a foreign culture, onto our agenda. Although Skid Row exists only about 10 miles from Pasadena, and only a few blocks from where many parishioners work, it represents a hidden community of people.

The contrast could not be more stark between life as we know it and love it, and life as we see it within these 50 square blocks in the heart of Los Angeles.

If you travel through Skid Row at night you look down the side streets and even the main streets, and you see hundreds of people huddled under cardboard and blankets on the hard pavement. At some places it's a bit like Colorado Boulevard on New Year's Eve, except that people are here endlessly rather than for a night, and they are here out of necessity rather than by choice. You make your way around the "bodies"—almost literally the "bodies"—of the addicted and the despairing. The life and the hope flow out of people before your eyes. Drugs and sex are available outside your front door. And after the drugs are purchased, users routinely go into the alley behind our hotel to use them. Muggings go unreported because they are so common here.

And at night you look down the alleyways—this is the

image that has been most shocking to me—you look down the alleyways of America, and you see the little bonfires lit to provide some warmth, and you wonder if these children of God, these brothers and sisters, will ever again know what it is to live in a home and to be surrounded by family and friends. And you remember your human link to these lives and situations that seem so foreign to you: these people also were born of mothers and fathers; they are children of hope and ambition; they bear deep within themselves dreams for their own fulfillment and instincts for love and sharing.

Of the 11,000 people on Skid Row, the vast majority are kind people, who only want a modest and safe place in which to live, who can pay us the $225 a month for rent gladly in exchange for cleanliness and cheerfulness and warmth. We want to preserve Skid Row for these people, because this is their last resort for housing and social services. We can't pretend that they will just disappear if we demolish their living space. We can't allow our residents to be terrorized by drugs and violence and injustice.

Some of you are surprised to know that we are trying to save Skid Row, rather than let purely commercial interests tear it down! The problem with tearing down the single room occupancy housing—the hotel settings where poor people take up permanent residence in a single room with no kitchen facilities, and a common bathroom down the hall—the problem with tearing down these old, substandard hotels is that no one is building substitute housing, no communities across America are welcoming these people, many of whom are elderly and disabled and with total incomes of between $300 and $650 a month. So All Saints Church and Leo Baeck Temple have decided, with others, that Skid Row must be preserved as a residential community, that the hotels must be renovated, that humane management must replace slum landlords, that the streets must be cleaned up, that the criminal elements who prey upon the vulnerable people of Skid Row must be dealt with, that the environment must be changed.

This is a tall order, and one wonders why nice congregations like All Saints and Leo Baeck have gotten involved in these messy, intractable problems. And why has a nice boy like Bill Doulos, the living antithesis of a street-smart, savvy person, become resident staff to this project?

When I look out my window onto my Main Street neighborhood, I wonder if even Mr. Rogers might have been a better choice!

When I first decided to move to downtown Los Angeles, the initial crisis was how to break this news to my Mother. Some of you know Miriam Lane, because she comes out from Pittsburgh to visit me once a year, and you love her almost as much as I do.

Now my Mother's mission in life for the past 46 years has been to keep me from doing things that are stupid. So I knew it would take quite a bit of courage on my part to call her up, but I tried to think of the positive side as I rehearsed my speech. The hotel is on Main Street, and that sounds very mainstream American. I would be living just five blocks from City Hall and the *Los Angeles Times*, and just down the street from the new Ronald Reagan State Office Building.

At the end of my long phone call home I felt relieved, pleased with my own frankness and with my mother's surprising acceptance. My only fear now is that if she ever finds out this hotel is on Skid Row...

She is flying out to see me at the Open House for the new Union Station/Depot facility in the fall of 1989. So I have about six months before my mother arrives to transform Skid Row into the humane and decent place I know it can be.

I've never been involved with a project where there has been more potential for failure. I feel as the captain of a ship, making my way through treacherous waters, with a chance to sink in the middle of the ocean, and with an equal chance to make port. In either case, I want to be on board. My knowledge won't make much of a difference, because when I went to school I studied theology and ethics when I should have been studying hotel management and construction finance. But I have the hope that the compassionate presence of the people of God might make a difference.

What are the many ways in which we desperately need to succeed?

One of the reasons that the All Saints-Leo Baeck project must succeed is that we are providing a model for other congregations and private non-profit agencies to enter this arena with us and to help us change the urban landscape of America. Alice Callaghan, the Skid Row Housing Trust and others engaged in the work want to see ten hotels a year undergo the same facelift and infusion of morality, so that what we hope will become the "Miracle on Main Street" can be duplicated. And while we are at it, we want to change the moral climate of America, so that poor people are no longer seen as an alien subculture of moral and economic failure, deserving of benign neglect, ostracism, condescension and punishment. Our presence at Fifth and Main is a signal that these realities of American life are going to be aggressively challenged by the opposite realities of the Kingdom of God.

Will the project succeed financially? From start to finish this is a $7-million endeavor, involving three buildings that are from 75 to 100 years old and funding from a variety of sources: the Community Redevelopment Agency of Los Angeles, the State of California, the State and National Tax Equity Funds, the Local Initiative Support Corporation, private donors and foundations and commercial lenders. We are on a financial roller coaster that dips and rises wildly—one day our budget is balanced and the next we have a construction change order that totals $100,000 in additional work. Where will we come out financially at the end of 1989?

Can Skid Row really be saved and changed—both the physical environment and the people? One year from now will our hotels represent an oasis of dignity and hopefulness for 100 people? And can the presence of this island of caring radiate some warmth to the surrounding neighborhood?

Can people who have lost hope and become alienated from society be swayed by the presence of encouragement and friendship? Can they believe once again in cleanliness and equanimity (and sobriety in some cases), and in the goodness of creation and of God?

And personally, can I maintain my own hopefulness and confidence? At this time next year, will life for me still be filled with good humor and excitement?

It's possible, of course, that our project could succeed in all of these areas, could succeed at the corner of Fifth and Main, and yet fail within our own lives. Will we take ownership of it, and put our own faith and resources on the line to see it succeed? Will members of the Church and Temple become involved personally as volunteers and participants in our social service program for our residents—offering the services of doctors and lawyers, accountants and counselors, providing friendship and advocacy, joining us for weekly potlucks with our residents in our community kitchen, driving people to the Social Security office or to the grocery store—or will we remain at a polite geographical and psychological distance?

I love to sort my way through the moral ambiguities of life. I seem to sleep better at night the more I encumber myself with insoluble dilemmas. I thrive spiritually when I am inundated with my own inadequacies. So you can imagine that I have an overwhelming serenity about my present posture in life—one foot at the corner of Fifth and Main and one foot at 132 N. Euclid—trying to bring two worlds that I love together. Not trying to save one at the expense of the other—that would be such a false reading of our situation.

What are nice congregations like Leo Baeck and All Saints doing on Skid Row? In addition to all the altruistic reasons that I have cited above, we are also trying to find meaning for our own lives, a secure sense of our own wellbeing in the hands of God; we are working out our own salvation; we are engaging in the most ancient tradition of our Judaeo-Christian heritage: like the Israelites wandering for forty years in the wilderness, we are searching for our own place of blessing in the Kingdom of God. That's what we are doing on Skid Row.

Can we bring the corporate faith of this Church and this Temple into the Skid Row arena? Can our hope flourish there?

I've always wanted to press the issue of faith. I've known for many years the God of my home and my upbringing. I knew God when I went to college and when I went to work. God sustains me in my ministry at Pasadena's Union Station. Now I want to know God on Skid Row. Don't you also want to press the issue, to subject your hope to the most rigorous testing, to discover whether it is the greenhouse variety of hope that withers away in the real world, or whether it is the genuine Messianic hope of the resurrection, that can conquer the terror that surrounds us and that can reverse the forces of injustice?

When I was just out of college, I was a member of a church group that believed in healing in a sophisticated kind of way. And every month we had a "healing" service and people came up to be forgiven and encouraged. One day at that service I took the invitation quite seriously and quite literally.

There was one fellow in our group, a friend of mine, who was crippled by multiple sclerosis. And I was sitting next to him when the altar call came for those who wanted to be cured. And I had an impulse and whispered to him, "Do you want to go up?"

And he said, "Yes." So I gathered him up into my arms and carried him forward while everyone stared in utter disbelief. I myself was skeptical, but I wanted to press the issue of faith.

My friend was not healed that night, and to the best of my knowledge he is not healed today. Maybe I shouldn't have carried him, maybe he should have lurched to the altar under his own initiative. Maybe it was the "utter disbelief" of the audience or my own skepticism. And we must say, at least for the record, with great respect, maybe...God is not God.

That is an unthinkable prospect, yet I think about it and

I therefore press the issue of faith. Skid Row, as it is at present, is also unthinkable, and God and Skid Row cannot coexist forever in the same city. So as a people of faith we have had this good impulse, to gather up Skid Row, to gather up the corner of Fifth and Main into our arms, and carry it to God.

Rabbi Sandy Ragins tells me that the Jews have a phrase to denote their mission in life: *tikkun olam*—healing the world. We are giving God a chance, and God is giving us a chance, to prove that our faith is both genuine and well-placed, that together we effect *tikkun olam*, and heal the world.

Some of you have suggested that there is an element of risk and heroism in what we do together on Skid Row. My response to that is, "I hope so." Ever since I read the story of David and Goliath when I was in Sunday School, I have thought that life, for an individual and for an institution, was synonymous with risk and heroism. We have no choice but heroism if we want to combat the forces at work in our society. It's amazing what a slingshot of faith, along with seven million stones, can do against the Goliaths of homelessness, addiction, violence and despair.

But let me share with you my concept of heroism.

There is a story of an ancient army which had established itself as the most formidable fighting force of its day. And the soldiers in this army marched shoulder to shoulder into battle, as they did in those days, following the lead of a legendary general. The army had a young recruit who was very ambitious for his country, and he visited the General one day and said to him, "General, I consider it a great honor to serve under your command. But I'd like, sir, not only to be a member of your army, but to be a hero."

"Can you tell me, General, how I can serve with such distinction?"

The young man thought he might be sent off on some dangerous mission, or be asked to undertake an extraordinary assignment. But instead the General said to him, "Two things must be done to become a hero in my army: keep your place in line, and pay attention!"

I've been at All Saints Church for 15 years. And for 15 years worth of Sundays, I've processed and recessed down and up the aisle with my colleagues on this staff, in the midst of the people of this Parish. I've heard the Gospel readings week after week, and I've paid attention to the sermons and sung the music and passed the kiss of peace.

What do you suppose happens to a person who is loved by God and encouraged by friends, who is shaped by the Gospel message and challenged by the prophetic witness, who for 15 years is forgiven and made whole through the sacraments of God's church? Don't you know how powerful your love is?

We are all broken people, who limp through life in many ways. And I limp right along in line with the rest of you. Yet some of you are among the best fathers and mothers in America. Some of the finest daughters and sons. Some of my friends are among the outstanding teachers and public servants, doctors and lawyers, business leaders and professionals, students and laborers and journalists. What a privilege to be among you!

Did you not expect me to become, almost by osmosis, the best social worker I could become? I always thought you wanted me to be a hero. Did you not expect me to represent the people of faith with as much diligence as I could bring to the most difficult challenge I could find?

For 15 years at All Saints Church I've kept my place in line and I've paid attention.

And so we journey together to Skid Row. We are creating in the midst of unbelievable despair and loneliness a safe place of caring and dignity.

As people of faith we must declare that the future is open as to whether we can heal the wounds of urban America. The jury is still out as to whether we can do our part to gather up the world and carry it to God. But if we want to find out how brilliantly the light of our faith shines, we take it into the darkest corner of the world.

So we journey together to Skid Row. Not so much you and I together, not so much All Saints Church and Leo Baeck Temple together, but the people of faith together with the God of our faith, the God who is our origin, our destination, and our companion for all of life's journey.

www.ingramcontent.com/pod-product-compliance
Lightning Source LLC
Chambersburg PA
CBHW050826160426
43192CB00010B/1917